I0406944

The Resistance
United in Love

The Resistance Authors:

Danielle Allen, Dylan Allen, JC Andrijeski, Megan Benjamin Evans, Natasha Boyd, Elizabeth Burgess, Deborah Cunningham Burst, Emme Burton, M.C. Cerny, Selene Chardou, S. Simone Chavous, T. Thorn Coyle, Sarah M. Cradit, Ella Dominguez, Nicole Falls, John Gregory Hancock, Bayli Lane, Robin Lee, Olivia Linden, G. Miller, Harper Miller, Morgan Jane Mitchell, C. Ricketts, Katherine Rhodes, Kimberly Rose, Amalie Silver, M. Stratton, Leslie Claire Walker, and Zoe York

The Resistance, United in Love

Copyright 2017

Each individual piece is copyrighted by that author listed here and on their individual piece(s): Danielle Allen, Dylan Allen, JC Andrijeski, Megan Benjamin Evans, Natasha Boyd, Elizabeth Burgess, Deborah Cunningham Burst, Emme Burton, M.C. Cerny, Selene Chardou, S. Simone Chavous, T. Thorn Coyle, Sarah M. Cradit, Ella Dominguez, Nicole Falls, John Gregory Hancock, Christina C Jones, Bayli Lane, Robin Lee, Olivia Linden, G. Miller, Harper Miller, Morgan Jane Mitchell, C. Ricketts, Katherine Rhodes, Kimberly Rose, Amalie Silver, M. Stratton, Leslie Claire Walker, and Zoe York

Cover by Q Design

The Resistance and its authors are independent entities and are not affiliated with the ACLU.

One hundred percent of the proceeds from the sale of The Resistance United in Love will go to the ACLU.

The Resistance United in Love is not affiliated with any political party.

ISBN: 978-1543178104

We the people
Will not be silenced
Our voices are important.

We the people
Will not be pushed aside
We will be seen
Our numbers are more than you know.

We the people
Will make a difference
We will hold the government accountable
Our empathy is not a weakness.

In these turbulent times we the people will stand together in the face of hate knowing we are all equal, and every life matters.

We the people are The Resistance, United in Love

Dedication

The Human Race

Forward

Forward

Since the 2016 election results, I have been trying to think of something to do, something that would make a difference. On International Holocaust Remembrance Day, while reading stories of firsthand accounts, I realized how much these stories can touch us and how relevant they still are today. Moved by Anne Frank and the bravery in her words, I remembered that the best lessons in history often come from real accounts that illuminate the humanity of tragic events in the past. Unlike the historian's viewpoint, a personal journey speaks to the moment and reveals what was most important to the people.

Writing, I knew, was something constructive I could do. And I knew plenty of other people who could write too. Others who were feeling the same powerlessness I felt. We could come together and be stronger for it. These are volatile times in which we live, and it seems we all have friends and family on opposite ends of the spectrum. Some who are willing to discuss openly and respectfully even if they disagree, and those who refuse to listen to a single word from the opposing side.

The first call I made was to Danielle Allen, an author whom I admire and with whom I had worked with in the past. In fact, we had just finished publishing a collaborative project together. I contacted Danielle to run the idea by her and get feedback. She became the first author to sign up. Little by little, we began to contact other authors who we knew felt the same way, and soon, The Resistance: United in Love, the anthology was born.

Without the generosity of Amy Queau, the cover designer, Katherine Rhodes for formatting the ebook and paperback, this wouldn't have been possible. To Sarah M. Cradit for contacting the charity and to all of the authors who donated their invaluable time and talent, we can guarantee that one hundred percent of the proceeds from this project will go to charity.

This book contains our real emotions, opinions, observations, fears, and also our hopes. By doing this collaboration, United in Love, we hope to show that *together*, we are always stronger.

No matter how many times we are told to sit down and shut up, we will rise and continue to stand up for what is right. To make this world a better place, with liberty and justice for all.

#TheResistance

Thank you,

M. Stratton

Empathy

By M. Stratton

To be a brilliant actor you must feel. You must put yourself in your character's shoes, in their life, find their motivation. Otherwise, your performance will be flat.

To be a great author you must open yourself up to the human emotion and pour it all out into the story you create out of nothing. You need to embrace the places you are scared to go in the real world.

Do not tell us to sit down and shut up. It is our empathy that makes these creations come to life.

We tell the stories, the interworking's of people's souls, what drives them to do the things they do.

We are the reason you are moved to tears, or laughter, or thoughtfulness.

We show you another way people have lived, loved, and died.

Do not tell us to sit down and shut up as we feel the pain of so many who are suffering.

We feel their loss,

We feel their joy.

We feel their hopelessness,

Their desperation.

And most of all, their hope.

This is what keeps us moving forward to go to the places that are so hard to look at, or brutally honest.

This is what makes us stand up with them to let them know their lives, their stories matter and need to be shared.

All of them.

Not some,

Not just the ones you agree with,

Or look like you.

But all. Because in the characters we bring to life, we are all of them.

For who?

By Danielle Allen

This isn't new. This is America. And this is the problem.

Racism isn't new.

Sexism isn't new.

Elitism isn't new.

Xenophobia isn't new.

Homophobia isn't new.

Discrimination as a whole is not new.

Although I'm glad to see so many people outraged at the injustices that are happening right now with the current climate of disregard for human rights and civil liberties, this is not new. Hate and oppression have been the thread holding the fabric of America together.

When people, the current administration (45) and his supporters in particular, talk about making America "great again" or returning to "American values," I can't help but feel sickened.

So I ask… making America great again? For who?

For the Natives whose land and people were pillaged at the inception of what we now call America? For the Native people who, even though they were here first, were forced onto reservations? For the first inhabitants of this land who have to fight to keep the government from tainting their water supply? How does one "make America great again" for the ONLY individuals who didn't come here as immigrants, refugees, or as victims of abduction and enslavement?

So again I ask… making America great again for who?

For the Africans who were kidnapped and forced into slave labor? For the Africans turned Americans who were born into a system of slavery, separated from their families, beaten, raped, tortured, and held in captivity? For the Americans of African descent who were denied access to education, forced to endure harsh conditions, and upon being "freed" from slavery, given nothing? How does one "make America great again" for the Americans who were deemed three-fifths of a person and received unequal access to education, opportunities, advancements, and resources? How does one "make America great again" for the Americans who have been treated unjustly by laws, law makers and law enforcers with the intention of perpetuating racial inequality and oppression from America's inception to present day?

Making America great again for who?

For women, who literally birthed us into existence, yet, even now, continue to fight men in power regarding what can and cannot be done to her own body? For the women who get paid less than their male counterparts for doing the same job? For the women who are often told they have to look a certain way because of the unrealistic beauty ideals that are established largely to satisfy the male gaze? For the women who are still being told that sexual assault and rape is their fault because of their behavior, sexual history or choice of outfit? How does one "make America great again" for the Americans who have historically been treated as "the weaker sex," property to be dominated, and sexual objects to be conquered?

Making America great again for who exactly? At what specific time in history are we supposed to get on board with returning to?

A time when same sex couples didn't have the rights to marry and adopt? Because someone wants to dictate what constitutes love and how love should look.

A time when the more money one earns means being taxed less and offered bailouts while complaining about welfare? Because someone decided receiving government assistance is only wrong if you're poor and you need it.

A time when the second largest religion in the world is demonized for the despicable acts of a few? Because if someone wanted to go after terrorists, they would target terrorists—all extreme terrorists, including the KKK—and not an entire religion because of a small extremist group.

A time when Americans are attacked daily—in the news, on television, in movies, in advertisements, in music, in everyday life—with images, words, and harmful propaganda painting people of color as inferior and invisible through lack of representation, negative stereotyping and sexual fetishizing to create distasteful caricatures that American people devour with their eyes and ears? Because there's no better way to demoralize, corrupt, and denigrate a group of people than to use psychological warfare—create conditions that stunt growth, convince them they can't do better, and watch the self-fulfilling prophecy unfold.

The list of reasons why America was never great for most of Americans could go on, but the point still remains: when they say "make America great again," it is unclear to which time period that they are referring. But it is very clear, what is meant by it.

Injustice, inequality, and bias have always been alive and well in America, but current laws were put in place to circumvent it. We'd made a little progress, but we weren't there yet. And with the current administration's objective to "make America great again," we are clearly moving in the wrong direction. Because making America great again seems to be code for not only undoing the progress that has been made, but returning to a more blatantly hateful, oppressive time.

And I have an issue with that.

At this point, we are beyond politics. What's happening right now is about equal rights, human rights, social justice, and civil liberties.

Being both Black and a woman (neither of which I would change even if I could), there are so many obstacles from both a racism and sexism point-of-view that impact my life daily. Although it has been exacerbated by the openly racist and sexist administration (45), America was founded on the violence, hate and oppression that is swirling around now. The corruption was here from the beginning and it is the existence of and the benefit from a racist, sexist, elitist, homophobic, xenophobic, etc. mindset that allowed people to hear what the current administration was saying and silently accept or loudly agree to support said administration. The current administration is a problem. But the root of the problem was here long before they came along.

The problem is with the entire system.

America functions the way it does because of the people. And the people function the way they do because there is a system in place that rewards racism, sexism, elitism, etc. And until the system is dismantled, this divided states of America will continue to break down on a fundamental level.

What's happening now is not new.

We've seen it before. We've seen it time and time again. And if we keep letting people get away with it, it will only continue to get worse.

So even though this isn't new, we resist because injustice anywhere is a threat to justice everywhere. And this administration is a threat to us all.

Instead of the current administration holding on to the reigns of discrimination and oppression to "make America great again" for only one very specific group (wealthy, heterosexual, Christian, white men), all of us, regardless of race, class, gender, sexual orientation, religion, etc., need to step up so we can make America great (for all of us) for the first time.

Do You See Me?
Because I see you

Danielle Allen

Long, jet black lashes cage salty tears
From anger, hurt, and the sum of my fears
As you justify your silence and unspoken support
Of a biased administration and the rights they abort.

Your declaration of friendship and love for me
Is in complete contradiction of what I see.
Because if you support the hate that they spew
I wonder if you see me…
Because I see you.

Melanin soaked skin, soft to the touch
Made thick from discrimination, injustice, and such.
America should be united, yes, that is true.
But America treats me a lot different than you.

Your declaration of friendship and love for me
Is in complete opposition of what I see
Because if you support the injustice you view
I wonder if you see me…
Because I see you.

My country, I love it; the red, white and blue.
That doesn't mean I can't be critical, too.

My ears hear your silence, clear and loud
And I wonder if ignoring oppression makes you proud.

Your declaration of friendship and love for me
Is in complete denial of reality.
Because if you defend the evil that they do
I wonder if you see me...
Because I see you.

You can't support an oppressive regime.
And seriously think we're on the same team.
Any time you root for another's demise
You create discontent, so don't be surprised.

Your declaration of friendship and love for me
Is as if you're ignoring what's happening.
Because if you don't get what's going on, too,
I wonder if you see me...
Because I see you.

Privilege received based on the color of your skin
Or your gender, your lover, your country of origin.
When you benefit from rampant inequality
It creates the divide between you and me.
When you say that we're friends and that you love me
Do you not think of that when you blindly agree
With the hateful words and derogatory tone
Of an administration whose intentions were known?

Do you see me? Because I see you
And what I'm seeing is not the person I knew

From your apathy and acceptance of hate
To the idea that they will make America great.

Do you see me? Because I see you
And what I'm seeing can't be true.
We're better than this or at least we could be
If you'd open your eyes, maybe you'd see.

qr

About the author:

Danielle Allen is a contemporary romance novelist and a diversity in romance advocate. She believes in spreading love, resisting hate, and standing up for what's right.

Author's website:
www.amazon.com/author/danielleallen

A letter to my sons

By Dylan Allen

On November 9, 2016 America woke up. The country can no longer be in denial about the content of its character or what it values. As an immigrant, a black person, a woman, I have always known what the phrase "American Values" really means. Now, it seems everyone else does too.

All of the phrases we have been taught to be believe are part of our country's moral fabric "Liberty and justice for all," "All men are created equal," "Home of the free" – were only meant to apply to a certain group of people. The documents that were drafted as part of this nation's formation were only meant to protect some of us.

The United States of America's only claim to exceptionalism is that it was founded on an idea, and is not a state created out of any natural commonality. The idea is this: The principals of liberty, justice and the right to pursue your happiness are more important than anything else. That those guiding ideals can be a more lasting and far more equitable foundation for a country than language, culture or ethnicity. The American Dream can be achieved by anyone who comes here pursuing those ideals and through their embrace of them, becomes a contributor to the furtherance of them.

So, my children, I say this to you. I am the American Dream and you are too. Your claim to this country is just as strong as those who seek to deny you access to the joys of full citizenship. It may seem as though racism and intolerance won on November 9th, but it is actually in its nadir. The decent people in this country have woken up and are ready to defend the values that make this country exceptional. Every day, we have more allies who join us. WE are the majority. So, don't be disheartened, be emboldened.

You are living a moment of history that will require that you be engaged as a citizen. I will stand with you. I will put myself in the breach to defend what I *know* to be my right to be free and happy. Maybe Thomas Jefferson didn't mean for me to be a beneficiary of the Bill of Rights, but he is dead. And America is my home. Let's make "American Values" mean what it should. Let us work to improve the content of the character of the country we all love. It will not be easy. It will be messy and hard and require sacrifice. But, it will be worth it. I'll be fighting right alongside you.

Love,

Mom

qr

About the author:
Dylan Allen is a Texas girl with a serious case of wanderlust. When she isn't writing or reading, eating or cooking, she and her family are planning their next adventure.

Author's website: www.authordylanallen.com

The Dysfunctional Family We Are

By JC Andrijeski

I read somewhere that one good thing that's come of Trump's election win is that it's pushed people to read again.

I can believe it.

I know my own appetite for news has been voracious. I skim headlines, looking for policy changes and reversals. I read opinion pieces, essays of hope, essays of conspiracy and pessimism. I read personal experiences. I read analyses of economic and regulatory changes. I read fake news and analyses of fake news. I read message boards and comment sections.

All the while, I attempt to draw lines, to analyze, connect, paint coherent pictures out of whatever honest-to-god facts I can dig out of hyperbole and fear. It turns out the movie, *Men In Black*, was right about one essential truth in media: if you bury facts in enough nonsense, they become nearly invisible.

Which forces me to face an uncomfortable truth.

In the end, it comes down to us. It comes down to who we are as individuals, yes, but even more than that, it comes down to how much we believe in and care about and rely on those around us. History is full of stories of amazing individuals, but in all but a very few cases, their power came from their ability to move others.

In the end, we have to look to our fellow humans for help. Railing against institutions of various kinds will always hit a wall.

At some point, we have to turn our heads, look at the people standing next to us.

Some of those people make up those very same institutions we are railing against. Reporters. Senators. Artists. Actors. Musicians. Talk show hosts. Industry leaders.

But most of those people are the rest of us. Housewives. The guy in the cubicle next to you who chews really loudly but has a great laugh. The woman who delivers your mail wearing Hello Kitty earmuffs. The kid in the Misfits T-Shirt who makes your coffee. The bus driver who stops to wait for you when she sees you dashing after her in high heels. The security guard at the mall who is constantly cracking his knuckles and telling dirty jokes.

I'm a historian at heart and a stickler for truth, and I'll never stop reading. I'll never stop trying to sift fact from fiction, or trying to understand what's really going on. But if I don't start to see this collectivity, this thing that is "us" as the real story, cataloguing facts and railing against distortions are just mental exercises.

Moreover, on a humanitarian level, they're a waste of time.

We need one another. That's not an abstraction. It's the absolute truth of what it is to be human. It's not enough to be right. It's not enough to care about "issues." It's sure as hell not enough to know the truth, as this election has demonstrated repeatedly.

We have to care about real, flesh-and-blood people. We have to genuinely want our neighbors to succeed, to live in a beautiful, prosperous world along with us. We have to want that for *all* of our neighbors, not just the ones who think or look like us. We have to want it for the rich ones and the poor ones, for the ones we're jealous of and the ones who do things that make us want to bang their heads against a wall.

In my opinion, we're in this mess because we've forgotten that.

Collectively, I mean. As a nation.

This election to me symbolizes a turning point, one that's been in the works for a while but came into stunning, shocking relief before and after November 9th.

The enemy now truly is within. That's not a figurative reality, anymore—it's a literal one. Americans didn't vote against a particular candidate. We voted against one another. We voted against a whole segment of the United States we didn't like. I don't even just mean in regards to race, sexual preference or whatever other "special interest" group might anger some of us, although that's a part of it, certainly.

I mean we voted to directly harm our fellow citizens.

We voted against our wives, our mothers, our daughters, our brothers, our neighbors, our bosses, our bus drivers and baristas. We voted against people who write stories we like to read, for venturing opinions we didn't want to hear. We voted against those who report the news. We voted against those who make movies we like to watch. We voted against scientists who dedicate their lives to making the world safer and more interesting for all of us. We voted against people who try to keep us from being poisoned or cheated or killed by our water and air.

We voted against total strangers. We voted against the guy down the street who's super annoying about his veganism.

Those people, those enemies... they *are* our country. They are us.

In many ways, watching this election and its aftermath is like watching a big, unruly and opinionated family trying to light its own house on fire while everyone is still living in it.

I know the media makes this worse. I know politicians make this worse. I know some liberals are insufferable. I know some writers and actors and musicians and artists are pompous asses. I know some conservatives are racists, sexists and homophobic. I know people with an education can be dicks. I know young college students can be dogmatic and naïve. I know it's hard not to be jealous of those who have more, especially when you've worked your ass off your whole life and those rich cocksuckers don't even seem grateful for what they have.

But these assholes are our people.

Just like we can't choose our families, we can't choose our people. If we start kicking everyone out of our family who annoys us, we'll end up with an empty house. We'll end up that bitter woman with all the cats who yells at kids on Halloween. We'll end up the old guy at the rest home who complains no one ever comes to visit.

We'll end up alone.

So we need to continue to look up. We need to work to change those institutions and policies and rules we believe to be harmful or unfair. But if we get lost in the mess of screaming and shouting, facts and distortions, change and stagnation—if we start to lose hope—we need to remember to look to our left.

Look to our right.

Remember that we're home.

qr

About the author:

JC Andrijeski is a USA Today bestselling author of paranormal mystery, urban fantasy & supernatural suspense, often with a metaphysical bent. She's lived all over the United States as well as parts of Europe, Australia and Asia, and has a background in journalism and political history, with a Master's degree in the latter. She currently lives and writes full-time in Bangkok, Thailand, where she has a beautiful view of a Buddhist wat right outside her window.

Author's website: www.jcandrijeski.com

In a civilized land

By Megan Benjamin Evans

In a civilized land
If one struggles
We all struggle
My sisters
My brothers
We the people
Of humanity
Everyone deserves rights
Everyone deserves freedom

In a civilized land

We use our voice
To speak
For those who cannot
As the children
Suffer on foreign soil
Laying in the shallow
Graves of rubble
I feel this weighing
On my soul

I live in a civilized land

I want to take those children

Under my protective wing
Letting them know
There is someone who's here
Someone who cares
Warm meals
A roof over their heads
Letting kids be kids
To laugh and play
And not worry
Those of parents that perished
under the ruins of war

Leaders
Hear their cries
See these innocent
Destressed children
Starved children
A cluster of destroyed children

In our civilized world

People are voluntarily ignorant
Regardless of consequence
In a nation of immigrants

How do we sleep at night?

qr

About the author:

Megan Benjamin-Evans, author of Fleeting Heart: A Collection of Poetry, is a passionate poet and prolific audiobook narrator.

Author's website:
https://www.facebook.com/geekgirlwho/

Friends

By Natasha Boyd

My skin is pale and my eyes are blue
Yours are beige and brown
We laugh together at the same joke
And others look on with a frown

Your true passion is making music
I like stringing love stories
My words run from left to right
And yours scroll beautifully backwards

I sometimes remember to pray once a week
And really I should get on my knees
You pray five times every day
To the same God, but facing true East

I have a boy who walks to school
Your son can do math in his head
Our children give us both joy and fear
And keep us awake in our beds

My other son likes trains and cars
Your daughter has the best smile to give
I want my kid to be a doctor one day
You want your children to live

About the author:

Natasha Boyd is a first generation immigrant. Her grandfather helped Jews flee Denmark, her mother left South Africa's apartheid, and now she wonders if she'll be detained on her next trip back into the bastion of the "free world", the USA. She also writes about LOVE, and important, but forgotten, WOMEN IN HISTORY. She rarely writes poems. As you can probably tell.

Author's website: www.natashaboyd.com

Human

by Elizabeth Burgess

Black. White. Arab American. Asian. Native American.

Hispanic. Straight. Gay. Lesbian. Bisexual. Queer.

Transgendered. Handicapped. Disabled. Veteran.

Mother. Father. Brother. Sister. Aunt. Uncle. Children.

Christian. Muslim. Buddhist. Jew. Atheist. Human.

Human. Human. Human. Human. Human. Human.

Human. Human. Human. Human. Human. Human.

Human. Human. Human. Human. Human. Human.

Human. Human. Human. Human. Human. Human.

Human. Human. Human. Human. Human. Human.

Human. Human. Human. Human. Human. Human.

Human. Human. Human. Human. Human. Human.

Human. Human. Human. Human. Human. Human.

Human. Human. Human. Human. Human. Human.

Human. Human. Human. Human. Human. Human.

Human. Human. Human. Human. Human. Human.

Human. Human. Human. Human. Human. Human.

Human. Human. Human. Human. Human. Human.

Human. Human. Human. Human. Human. Human.

Human. Human. Human. Human. Human. Human.
Human. Human. Human. Human. Human. Human.
Human. Human. Human. Human. Human. Human.
Human. Human. Human. Human. Human. Human.
Human. Human. Human. Human. Human. Human.
Human. Human. Human. Human. Human. Human.
Human. Human. Human. Human. Human. Human.
Human. Human. Human. Human. Human. Human.
Human. Human. Human. Human. Human. Human.
Human. Human. Human. Human. Human. Human.
Human. Human. Human. Human. Human. Human.
Human. Human. Human. Human. Human. Human.
Human. Human. Human. Human. Human. Human.
Human. Human. Human. Human. Human. Human.
Human. Human. Human. Human. Human. Human.
Human. Human. Human. Human. Human. Human.
Human. Human. Human. Human. Human. Human.
Human. Human. Human. Human. Human. Human.
Human. Human. Human. Human. Human. Human.
Human. Human. Human. Human. Human. Human.
Human. Human. Human. Human. Human. Human.
Human. Human. Human. Human. Human. Human.
Human. Human. Human. Human. Human. Human.
Human. Human. Human. Human. Human. Human.

Human. Human. Human. Human. Human. Human.
Human. Human. Human. Human. Human. Human.
Human. Human. Human. Human. Human. Human.
Human. Human. Human. Human. Human. Human.
Human. Human.

Human. Human. Human. Human. Human. Human.
Human. Human. Human. Human. Human. Human.
Human. Human. Human. Human. Human. Human.
Human. Human. Human. Human.

Human.

qr

About the author:

Elizabeth lives with her partner in their beloved Louisiana. Her favorite things are writing about topics that make people blush, photography, and standing up for what's right. She also loves the color black.

Author's website: www.liddyburgess.com

Carrying the Torch of Freedom

By Deborah Cunningham Burst

"A bull contents himself with one meadow, and one forest is enough for a thousand elephants; but the little body of a man devours more than all other living creatures." Seneca the Younger, c. 64

Tootling around in my first car, the patriotic-blue Pinto, I plastered a peace sign on the back windshield. The logo had a blue-green earth with a red peace sign burned through the center. Some may think, "another '70s freedom-reeking anti-war sticker," but it was more, it was a time of protest, a time of reckoning. We, my generation, were fighting to save our people and our planet.

And we won. After much protest President Nixon ended the Vietnam War and in December 1970, the EPA (Environmental Protection Agency) was born.

Yes, I was a flower child. I loved walking in the woods and tubing in freshwater streams. And yes, I'm still a tree hugger and very proud of it. Joni Mitchell was among my spiritual leaders in her rally to stop deforestation. Her battle cry still rings true in her song Big Yellow Taxi, "you paved paradise and put up a parking lot…"

And the battle rages on.

Dollars and developers rule this country. They rape virgin forests destroying trees that filter our air and home to vast species of wildlife. They are replaced with temples of concrete and empty strip malls. As a consequence, it is hard working citizens that pay the price with devastating floods sweeping away homes and businesses.

How ironic that the same politicians that don't believe in Climate Change proudly sing the song, "America the Beautiful." Katharine Lee Bates wrote the song more than a hundred years ago motivated by the beauty of Colorado's Pikes Peak: "her spacious skies, amber waves of grain and purple mountain majesties."

And the same song reminds us, "Till selfish gain no longer stain, The banner of the free!"

But many in Washington ignore this century-old plea; instead they grumble that the country is drowning in regulations. It's a repeated roar fueled by elected elitists and the oil company's silver-tongued lobbyists. Together they are chipping away at the EPA slashing $800 million from its funding and censoring their website, while others are lobbying to eliminate the EPA altogether.

And I cry. Just when I think a human being can cry no more, a flood of tears continues to fall, but with every tear comes anger.

Millions share the same frustration and with it comes a resurrection, a renewed energy to fight. Just as the enemy believes they have silenced the so-called maligned marchers, we rise again in peaceful protests. We are a solidarity armed with poetic posters damning the wicked ways of greedy government.

And we will never stop until justice prevails.

But yet there are naysayers, blinded by false hope, lies upon lies. Have they become insensitive to our environment, zombie-like robots cloistered in their high-tech vehicles?

The late award-winning author Walker Percy called it an aesthetic realm, the happy consumer who builds their pompous identity through materialistic means?

Percy predicted what he coined the "Hurricane Theory." He envisioned a time when the government no longer serves its people; it is then the people come together breaking free from the bonds of social hierarchy to help their fellow man.

And so the storm has come, this is our destiny, a time of reckoning.

People from across the world have joined hands demanding equal rights for all, to rid the world of dictators and save us from ecological damnation.

But there's more…

I fight in memory of my brother, Skip Cunningham, who died of AIDS at the age of 29.

I get teary-eyed when I pick up that sign, carrying my brother's torch for equal rights.

Skip was part of the Second National March on

Washington, a political rally at our nation's capital on October 11, 1987. His doctor told him the march would shorten his life. And it did, he died two weeks after his return.

He and 750,000 peopled joined the LGBT community and all those stricken with AIDS demanding President Regan acknowledge the AIDS crisis and dedicate more funds in research for its cure.

Skip's country failed him, his employer failed him, his doctors failed him, his church failed him, and even the hospitals failed him. They moved AIDS patients to wards with no call buttons waiting for them to die.

It puts a fire in you that will never die. This fight is for you Skip; I will continue the fight, your fight, and our fight.

Together all of us will conquer the hellish darkness that binds us and break free to a new world order, the dawning of a bright future filled with a global community and the magic we all bring.

History Does Repeat Itself

By Deborah Cunningham Burst

If you live long enough you begin to notice a pattern, no matter your intellect in politics, no matter pre or post Internet, it all becomes clear. History does repeat itself, but it's what we learn along the way that makes a difference.

Now in the sixth decade of my life, I remember those moments, that time when life stood still, when the real world stepped on stage.

It was 1963 and we were a Navy family living in Bermuda with minimal daytime television, except for November 22, 1963. Walking home from school, I opened the door with my usual jabbering and heard the television. Only eight-years old, it is a moment forever etched in my mind, my mother was kneeled on the floor sobbing with head in hands.

Standing in disbelief, trying to catch my breath, the sound of the television seemed a million miles away. She told me that President Kennedy had been shot and killed. I kneeled down caressing her, my face nuzzled against her neck and together we cried a flood of tears. It was an awakening and intro to the tragedies of life.

Back in the states, finishing up junior high and looking forward to high school, 1968 was a year ripe with blood and protests. Every day the news repeated the escalation of the Vietnam War and racial riots in the street. I did my best to drown the noise in my pink bedroom listening to Beatle songs and lip-syncing "To Sir With Love."

But I soon realized you grow up fast when the world around you begins to crumble.

And so it began, Martin Luther King, Jr. was assassinated on April 4 and Robert Kennedy on June 6. Both were masters in bringing peace, both advocating equal rights, and both killed in their prime.

I grew up in a world that taught children to hide under their desks during the Atom-bomb drills. I grew up in a world where girls were second-glass citizens. I grew up in a world where blacks were regulated to separate bathrooms and balcony-only seats in movie theaters. And even though I tried my best to escape the world, the world came to me. I grew up in a world with racial riots in school.

Among my first days of high school, a fight began and went out of control. Teachers tried their best to gather students and rush them into the classrooms. We were ordered to stay under our desks and away from the windows for fear of broken glass. But I could hear the screams, the shrills of pain, I had to see it, I decided it was time to immerse myself, time to see the truth.

It was a racial riot, whites and blacks beating each other, the blood pouring down their faces, many with torn shirts falling off their chests. And there were chains, so many chains, that's what I remember the most, the fierce brutality of the chains swinging in the air. I was forever changed that day.

For the last thirty years I have fought political injustice, be it their actions to pollute this planet or take away our rights, I'm not shy in holding signs and speaking my peace.

Many people have been complacent in their charge against political factions, most too busy raising families and making a living. But things have changed. Donald Trump has inflicted pain and suffering, but Donald Trump has also ignited a war among peaceful protestors.

In the past, politicians were often greeted at town hall meetings with sparse attendance but now they are packed with angry voters. Trump has awakened a sleeping giant.

Just three weeks after Donald Trump took office, the "orange crush" turned a new shade—RED. His blatant lies, cynical taglines and campaign chants may have worked on the campaign trail, but now reality has smacked Trump across the face.

His illegal immigration ban, which was struck down by the courts, was probably the one act that truly defined Trump's administration. They promised to turn the country around, and it seems they are doing just that, bringing the country back to the days of racism, flashbacks of my childhood.

It's the same words spoken by the likes of Russia, Trump is committed to dividing the country based on race and ethnicity, closing the U.S. borders, and literally isolating Americans to build a new world order. But the opposite has happened.

Protests across the globe have joined their American brothers and sisters. Recently tens of thousands have hit the streets across the United Kingdom protesting an upcoming Trump visit. In an article by Jon Stone, a political correspondent with the Independent, he reported that a Stop Trump Coalition has been formed filled with civic leaders, trade unions, journalists and celebrities.

They march in protest against President Trump, calling him a "racist and misogynist using his power to divide." Across the UK they vowed to bring millions of marchers in protest of Trump's policies and their government's collusion with Trump.

Although history stands to repeat its wicked ways, electronic media and communication has come to our rescue. The rise of this administration and the ensuing fight will truly be one for the history books. One studied by the scholars of social science for decades.

So yes, history does repeat itself. Just as the masses came together to fight Hitler's ethnic genocides, today's global army of peaceful protestors is united with an arsenal of weapons. Not as glitzy as a fire-breathing dragon perhaps, but equally effective—passion, the media and the Internet.

The question is, who will be our next JFK, our Martin Luther King, Jr., our Robert Kennedy? Who will emerge as our leader?

qr

About the author:

Deborah Burst is a New Orleans native who enjoys writing outdoors at her home in Mandeville, Louisiana. In her 15-year career as a freelance writer and photographer she has published more than 1,000 articles and twice as many photographs on a local, regional and national level. She has written four books in four years featuring historic churches and cemeteries.

Author's website: www.deborahburst.com

To My Boys: February 5, 2017

By Emme Burton

Ian and Sean,

There have been two other times that I thought to write a letter like this to you, but each of those times it never happened.

The first time was September 11, 2001. I sent you off to school with your dad, Ian, and took Sean with me to drop him off at daycare near work. You were 5 and 1 years old, respectively. On the way, the most unbelievable thing happened. The radio station I listened to every morning broke in and announced a plane had hit one of the World Trade Center buildings.

When the first plane hit, none of the reporters were speaking of terrorism, just how very odd it was. I took you, Sean, into daycare and kissed you good-bye. You toddled off to play with your friends, like it was any other day. But it wasn't. By the time I reached my desk at the hospital where I worked, the second tower had been hit, and everyone knew in their hearts this wasn't an accident.

America had been attacked. Think about those four words. America had been attacked. It seemed surreal. In my mind, the only attack on America was Pearl Harbor. My parents and grandparents spoke of it. Surely, this wasn't true.

I took care of patients and snuck peeks at the television in the sports gym, when there wasn't a patient there. All the therapists huddled around any source of information with mouths agape and watery eyes.

I called my husband to make sure he was okay. I called my mother. I called my father, who at the time worked for the government at a job with a security class high enough that I never knew quite what he did. When I called, I asked him if he knew what was going on. He told me, "I know as much as you do, but I wouldn't come down here (meaning the place he worked). You'd get a machine gun in your face." Without telling me, I knew his building, perhaps his whole compound, was on lock-down.

I moved through my workday in a fog, my only thoughts on picking up my baby and getting home to see my other baby and my love. It seemed the only safe place on earth.

Your dad and I fed you both and got you occupied with something and then went into the bedroom to watch the coverage. We didn't want to scare you. We watched the footage of the planes hitting the buildings, now including the Pentagon and the wreckage spread across a Pennsylvania field, over and over. Even our safe place, our home, seemed that it might not be safe.

The next few days were a blur. We lived our life, but more carefully, more quietly. The whole world was quiet. Not a plane in the sky. Less traffic on the streets. We were all home with our "people," watching as we came to grips with the fact that thousands of people had died and that the world, our world, would never feel the same again.

I never wrote you guys a letter then, because, even with the events that came after 9/11 or the wars and the renewed prejudice against people that even appeared to be vaguely Middle Eastern, to me, it felt like people were coming together, being just a little kinder. Cautious, but kinder. My world was small. My world was you and I needed to get on with the business of daily life and raising small children. I didn't look outside my circle. Perhaps I should have.

The second time was January of 2008. I don't need to elaborate to you. It was the worst month of my life during the worst year of my life. And my association, perhaps it was one of the worst years for you.

On January 16th, Grandpa Dave died after an almost three year battle with pancreatic cancer.

Eleven days later, your Uncle Pete took his life. You didn't know him very well, but his brain was sick and had been for a while and Grandpa's death was more than he could handle. So he went away.

I didn't write a letter then, because the year, to put it bluntly, went to shit.

Anxiety, earthquakes, a city hall shooting massacre in our town, and horrible illness were the events that made up that year.

It was all "saved" on a night in December, six days

before Christmas. Your dad agreed we could get a dog. We drove to Illinois and met a sweet Yorkie named Rocky, which we changed immediately to Jasper, and took him home.

I have distinct memories of bringing him home in the car, in the dark, passing by Christmas lights. Jasper whined and you boys and one of your friends sang Bob Marley's "Everything's Gonna Be Alright" to him. He calmed down and so did I. It was one of the first times I felt whole in 2008. Because of the two of you and a small dog.

But now, I am writing the letter.

It's February 5, 2017. We've had a new administration for a little over two weeks and I'm as on edge as I've ever been. I'm on edge at work. I'm on edge in public. I'm on edge when on Facebook. I don't know who to trust.

I miss my dad, your grandpa. I wonder what he'd make of all this. I don't trust our administration to protect me or your dad or you. I feel like everyone is a target.

Our new president and the people he's surrounded himself with, appear to have only their own interests and agendas at heart.

Let me re-phrase. I don't know who to trust except you boys, your dad and the like-minded people we encounter.

So, what I'm saying is, you are older now, you have your own hearts and minds and I'm proud to say they are wise and beautiful. You were born white, male and middle-class and have become kind, empathetic men that can see beyond yourselves. You see the mean-spiritedness and mental illness coming from a leader we were saddled with. I didn't point it out to you. You saw it on your own. I could not be more proud.

So far, I haven't moved on with the business of raising you like I did in 2001, because you are both pretty much "raised." I don't know what will happen next. I'm praying that this year is not another 2008. I wish a song or a moment could appear to calm my unease, but I'm not holding my breath.

I don't have a lot of advice except this: remain hopeful. It goes a long way. Keep talking about issues. Keep standing up for your truth. Keep writing, calling, and marching. It's what we can do.

We thc people.

Remain hopeful.

I love you so much,

Mom

qr

About the author:

Emme Burton is the author of the Top 50 RomCom SNACK, the Better Than Series and AWKwaRd, Victoria. She wants you to #resist #persist and shop at Nordstrom.

Author's website: www.emmeburton.com

Resistance.

By M.C. Cerny

I am a third generation born American. I am white. I am a woman. I am privileged. I am a daughter. I am a mother. I believe in a higher power greater than myself, but have no religious affiliation. I struggle with who I am.

Nothing is ever simple, and nothing should be judged at first glance.

I don't think there has been a time in my life when I wasn't fighting for something. My fights graduated from confronting the boys who will be boys on the playground to the disparities in the boardroom.

Resisting was my identity.

During the summer the year I turned twelve, my grandparents took me on a trip to visit family in Prague. It was part of a genealogy excursion my grandfather was taking to track our family history. It was that summer my life veered toward a different course when I learned where I came from.

My ancestors were Jews persecuted by the Romans. They changed our last name to identify us, to keep us in place. They became Catholic and disguised their synagogue on top of a hill. They buried religious artifacts among the vineyards and sunflower fields hoping to forget the past.

My ancestors transported indentured servants to the Americas. They thought they were honoring debts by selling human flesh. They owned plantations. There was a time they owned people.

I am a part of both sides of a complicated coin.

My ancestors fled Europe during the occupation under the Ottoman Empire. They were bankers, bread makers, and shipbuilders. They left everything behind.

My ancestors led an underground resistance in the Czech Republic under its occupation by the Nazis. They held meetings above the Secret Police headquarters in broad daylight. Cousins served on both sides decimating family ties to never speak again. For a second time, our name changed.

My ancestors were hunted by the Nazis because they were doctors. On vacation in Austria, they received word they would be taken on their return at the border because of their surgical skills to serve the Nazi Army. They fled in the night. Rolling their car over the Swiss border they left everything behind.

I am both proud and shamed.

How does one reconcile the good of one half with the bad of the other, for I am products of both?

I ask not to be judged for the actions of my ancestors,

but for the choices I make today. I will keep my faith in humanity. I will remain steadfast and hopeful.

I will keep resisting.

qr

About the author:

M.C. Cerny fell in love with books after experiencing her first real ugly cry reading, Where The Red Fern Grows. When M.C. is not writing, you'll find her lurking in Starbucks, running stupid marathon, singing Disney show tunes, and searching out the perfect shade of pink nail polish.

Author's website: www.authormccerny.com

A Caged Bird's Song

By Selene Chardou

Am I a piece of meat?
Something to beat?
Quiet and unseen?
Never to be unclean?
I have no rights.
Afternoon delights,
Exchanged for Putin's Orange Pig.
And at the trough, he scored big.
With bigots, racists – white and black,
Brown and pink, never looking back.
Some thought this through,
But the election was a zoo.
One that made the far right think time has turned,
That my grandfather can be again lynched and burned.
But I have a piece of news for these deplorable,
Yes, the word is awful and horrible.
You might think you have won
The bird in the cage won't ever write a song.
But we are many and we have might.
No matter what you think of me as a woman, I will
fight.
I'll take you down and not within a reality show,
In real life, you'll actually feel the blow.
Of my strength and my cry.
We will never die.

Women aren't just a piece of pussy,
Tits, ass and just something to look pretty
We are the givers of life and the Grim Reaper.
No, we aren't trash and the least bit cheaper,
Than Yves Saint Laurent, Chanel or Gucci,
Without us, where would the world be?

qr

About the author:

SE Chardou is the author of romantic suspense and psychological romance. She also writes under the names of Selene Chardou and Elle Chardou.

Author's website:
www.facebook.com/Selene.chardou.and.elle.chardou

Why Am I Afraid

By S. Simone Chavous

Some ask why am I afraid,
Insisting nothing will really change
The only reply to be made,
Things will never be the same.

My fear stems not from taxes,
Nor conservative policy
But from hate brandished like axes,
By those emboldened by this presidency.

It's not about the Democrats,
It's not about the Republicans
It's about so many turning their backs,
No longer concerned for their fellow man.

I fear for the sick,
For the differently abled
And for those unable to pick,
The cruel ways they'll be labeled.

Our great country once stood tall,
Known as a beacon of hope
Now it's known for an expensive wall,
Serving as the butt of a joke.

All lives matter they yell,

Down from their golden steeple
As they shut out the refugees,
And put pipes before people.

I'm afraid for my daughters,
As we put down this foundation
Marching their future to the slaughter,
What will become of this nation?

My fear shows me the dark,
But love brings a ray of light
Sister's voices ascending like the lark,
Sweet resistance fighting back the night.

To the resistance we must hold,
As we face the coming years
Fighting in the name of love,
Instead of giving into fear.

qr

About the author:

S. Simone Chavous is an International Best Selling
paranormal and contemporary romance author. When
she isn't writing, she enjoys reading, sketching, cooking,
running, and spending time with family. She lives in
northern Indiana with her family.

Author's website: www.ssimonechavous.com

We Did Not Gentle Go

By T. Thorn Coyle

Long years, comfort distracts, ignoring might,
Forever squashed inside the slumbering breast;
Until we woke, pow'r scattered in day's light.

There lived harrowing stories, laced with fright,
By those whom beastly jaws had rent apart;
Too easy to discount in creeping night.

Shot in the streets, shoved out, locked up by might,
Because they were not ours, our hands had stayed;
And then the deeds turned on us came to light.

And up we rose, with fists, placards, and sight
–Finally afflicted– cleared of comforting ways:
"Oh siblings! We will join you in this fight!"

Too little, then, perhaps, some said too slight,
But not too late, no never, join the fray!
To battle go, and fierce, to put things right.

Wild honesty and rage, reclaimed the might
Of people long held down, or under sway.
Rage, raging, against damaged, damning blight,
We did not gentle go, into the night.

qr

About the author:

T. Thorn Coyle is the author of "Like Water," the story collection "Alighting on His Shoulders" and the "The Panther Chronicles" series (Spring, 2017). She's also the author of multiple non-fiction books. A lifelong activist, she currently resides in the Pacific Northwest and drinks a lot of tea.

Author's website: www.thorncoyle.com

The World Cannot Afford My Silence

By Sarah M. Cradit

The world cannot afford my silence
History has shown me the cost
Which is greater than or equal to my own soul

My country cannot afford my silence
Our tired, poor, huddled masses yearning to breathe free
How soon we forget, we all were these things once

My conscience cannot afford my silence
I will not retreat to the comfort of my privileged life
While others are denied their inalienable right to the
same

My faith cannot afford my silence
Jesus said, as I have loved you, you are also to love one
another
There is no asterisk on another

The past cannot afford my silence
Millions of persecuted souls beg us to listen to their
sacrifice
We alone can ensure it was not made in vain

The present cannot afford my silence

Every generation has their moment of truth
Wisdom tells me this is ours

The future cannot afford my silence
Our actions today will be in the history books of
tomorrow
I am the descendant of a witch you failed to burn

qr

About the author:

USA Today Bestselling Author of Southern Gothic
Fantasy Fiction

Author's website: www.sarahmcradit.com

LEGACY

By Ella Dominguez

Legacy. It's a daunting word if I think about it too much. Defined as *something transmitted by or received from an ancestor or predecessor or from the past*, I'm left wondering what it is that this country's *legacy* will be. Will it be a legacy of love and acceptance, or of fear and intolerance? Sadly, it seems as though it will be the latter. What other conclusion can one deduce by the actions we've seen as of late? And what do I tell my daughter who is looking on at all of this with confusion? How can I answer her honestly when I myself am just as confused? I thought I lived in a world that was becoming better; in a world that was learning, albeit slowly, to accept everyone and all of their differences. Where has all of that change gone? Yet, I know there is hope. I have to believe that. I *need* to believe that. It's the only thing that makes my day to day life tolerable. It's all I have to offer my daughter. Love *will* prevail and the hard lessons learned from so many years ago in far off lands will shine through. It *has* to. The next four years will be the true test of time and will test the patience and morals of many, but so long as we stand strong, *together,* our country's people will prove to themselves and others that we are genuinely a kind and loving force to be reckoned with. It's easy to point a negative finger and complain, but it takes a person of integrity and strength to do something about that which they're complaining, and to say to themselves and those around them, "I am going to help make the change this country needs." And so, "I am going to help make the change this country needs." Will you? And what will *your* legacy be?

qr

About the author:

Mother, lover, dreamer and bestselling author, Ella finds comfort in ukuleles and unicorns. An avid reader above all else, she takes pleasure in writing the stories that the characters in her head tell her to.

Author's link: Www.facebook.com/theartofsubmission

Where Do We Go From Here:

A stream of consciousness ramble now that they mans is president...

By Nicole Falls

i.

It was a Tuesday, so it was trivia night. I sat in the bar with my friends K & D, our eyes glued to the many television screens around us tuned into various news stations tallying the vote counts instead of the normal variety of sports. "He can't win this," my friend K cried out multiple times. "There's no way he's got this," D replied, reassuringly.

[It is important that here I note that I am a Black woman in my mid-thirties and my two companions on that fateful night were White women—one in her mid-twenties, the other in her early thirties.]

The two of them were so confident that this country was better than electing this guy as our president. That our soon-to-be former commander in chief was proof positive that our country had made strides in its thoughts, actions, and behaviors. They wholeheartedly bought into President Barack Obama's "hope and change". Much like the refrain of the spirituals my ancestors once sang, they believed America had *overcome*.

As the night wore on, states kept turning red. At one point, I was full on gulping beer as Ohio then Michigan then Pennsylvania was called for him. Before we parted ways that night I joked, "It's been nice knowing you ladies—not sure if I'll be able to talk to y'all under that guy's regime. De jure segregation soon come!"

ii.

The first words I heard when I woke up on Wednesday morning were "President-elect [redacted]". I took the day after the election off from my every day job. Whether the results were in my favor or not, I just knew that I didn't want to be surrounded by people who were not politically astute pontificating about why Hillary Clinton or that guy from The Apprentice won the election. Despite going to bed having faced the fact that the dude most famous for uttering the words "You're Fired" on a reality television show would soon be in possession of the keys to the highest house in our land, it was a startling, numbing feeling to have it validated by many trusted news sources.

Hate had won. Bigotry prevailed. Ignorance ran rampant, whilst also being blissed for some. I was a mess of despair and ambivalence. I'd never held the hope of this country being better than...too many incidents in which my melanin denied me access, got me looked at in askance, or even worse straight up ignored for me to even think about better. But I'd certainly hoped we were slightly above the lowest common denominator. The election of this guy, by an electoral margin that still baffles me, will forever be an indelible stain on the history of this country.

iii.

I honestly cannot bring myself to say the words President and [his name] in succession. You'll notice over the course of this narrative I refer to him as this dude or that guy. I'm affording him a higher sense of respect here than I would in conversation with friends where he is bestowed a more...*colorful* moniker that calls to mind an incestuous act involving a maternal figure.

My thoughts on his regime so far, and what I envision a future in his America to be like? Much like this essay-- disjointed, bewildered, apprehensive, yet not despondent. I cannot afford to let fear rule me. It will only serve as an agent of paralysis, resulting in me letting life happen to me instead of being a proactive participant. Those who came before me fought against evils much worse than a comb over and orange spray tan. Their strength serves as a beacon, a guiding force that propels me to persevere and prevail.

qr

About the author:

Nicole Falls is a contemporary Black romance writer who has taken entirely too long to complete her first project. She's also a ceramic mug and lapel pin enthusiast who cannot function without her wireless Beats constantly blaring music. When Nicole isn't writing, she spends her time trolling her friends and family while drinking coffee and/or cocktails or checking off yet another of these great United States visited in her quest to see some land! She currently resides in the suburbs of Chicago.

Author's website: http://www.nicolefalls.com/books/

Words Are Stones We Hurl At Horrors

by John Gregory Hancock

resist

survive

overcome

persevere

rebuild

These were the words that fanned through my mind like a burning fire, and I struggled to tame them. Do I freeze them in an essay, or a poem, or blow them like embers into an anthem? I consider myself a crafter of words. I'm familiar with how to use them, how to coax the right ones out of their burrows.

But still and yet, words failed me.
Except those words:

resist

survive

overcome

persevere

rebuild

And then I knew why.

Because words are meant to fail us.

I remembered back to history's darkest knots, times blacker that any thought would ever be. Wars of greed, spoiled tyrants, careless dictators, and worse. Much worse.

Instinctively, men used words offered in the open hand, with clear faces. In defense. In hope. In desperation. Conciliatory words, supplicating words, frightened words, surrendering words.

But words are such insubstantial things. They can carry great concepts, but they themselves are so often trivial.

Of course, if what you throw them at is human, then rational thought can be a seed that takes shape, and changes a heart. If a government or a people are approaching humane, you might entreat them to ask for mercy, you may find just the correct, precisely crafted words, so that perhaps you can dissuade them.

Wearying time and wearingly again, diplomats have offered words like appeasing sops to monsters, only to have the brutish creature turn and rend.

Words are stones we hurl at horrors. In our minds, in our legal houses, in our parliaments. Tiny things, we can but string them together in chains of hope, in vain hope, to serve as shields. But when the knives of fascism swing, words are ripped asunder. Books are burned, thinkers are executed. Education is cast underfoot.

But the words that run through my heart --

resist

survive

overcome

persevere

rebuild

-- These are not mere words. They are, after close inspection, actions. They are instructions. They are a marching song. They are a plan, a blueprint, a fiery brand to look upon and not wither.

For if we falter, we are lost.

Monsters have no mercy. They never tarry in their juggernaut paths and shadows.
When waging war against the heartless, the cruel, the insane, the treacherous, or the evil, simple words alone cannot win the day.

RESIST
Become the countermeasure.

Mass in numbers

Use your intellect as well as your heart

Remember Evil runs down the same familiar gutters.

It signals its motives, writ large in hubris
(assuming we cannot fathom)

It is predictable.

Outsmart them.

The last thing they expect

is resistance.

SURVIVE

Live to tell

live to pass down truths

be present even in the massacre

shelter in the nooks

in the barren fields

gather all the hiding places

and build a sanctuary

to live and fight again

OVERCOME

Become greater

react stronger

adopt resilience

remain flexible and unpredictable

arm yourselves with justice,

plated with honor,

fortified with rational hope

Give comfort

Lend courage

PERSEVERE

never give up

You are on the right side of history

REBUILD
We must rebuild

the structures they have razed.

We must lift up

the souls they have downtrodden.

It is up to us, and no other

because they cannot be trusted

to clean up their own debris.

qr

About the author:

John Gregory is a storyteller, a graphic artist and a patriot who cares deeply about this country.

Author's website: http://www.johngregoryhancock.com/

All of Us

By Bayli Lane

This isn't about Trump being our president.

People who want to suppress the resistance make the protests sound trivial, petty, irrelevant. They do this by calling us snowflakes, whiners, and sore losers.

What they don't want to admit, refuse to acknowledge, or are simply afraid to see is that these protests mean so much more than simply not liking our POTUS.

It's the majority demanding democratic representation.

It's fighting against sexism because our pussies aren't there for men to grab. Women are worth more than a rapist's "twenty minutes of fun."

It's commanding equal rights for women. We should be making the same amount as a male with the exact position. My intelligence should be noted before my beauty.

It's shutting down racist and bigoted notions, and begging politicians to stand up for all ethnicities represented in our country.

It's rejecting the idea that only one religion is allowed here.

It's not allowing xenophobia to spread like a disease, demonizing anyone different is dangerous.

It's protecting our earth and the welfare of our children from deforestation, urbanization, industrialization, and pollution, and overall destruction of the environment.

It's all of us, coming together as one, and saying each and every one of us should have equal opportunity.

Race, Gender, Religion, Sexuality: none of these should impede our rights.

So, no. This isn't just about Trump being president.

We should protest.

Our president should be protecting *all* people of America.

Not just the ones who look like him.

qr

About the author:

Animal lover, social activist, and contemporary romance author.

Author's website:
https://www.goodreads.com/authorbaylilane

Clueless

By Robin Lee

Earlier in 2016, Trump was asked what he thought about the day-to-day operations of the presidency. His reply? "I don't think about it."

Um... A man who is running for POTUS doesn't think about what the actual daily responsibilities of the office will be? That right there should have been enough to give most people pause at accepting him as a viable candidate. Unfortunately, it did not.

Cut to November 2016 and a couple of days after Trump won the Electoral College and he meets with sitting President Obama - PEOTUS Trump seems genuinely surprised by how much responsibility he is about to undertake. Newt Gingrich is also quoted as saying Trump told him the job is bigger than he thought.

Given his earlier comment, it doesn't shock me that Trump is taken aback by the scope. Honestly, even those who have been in politics for years would probably also be a little surprised. However, ANYONE else who has aspired to become POTUS would have at least given some thought to what it would entail.

And now, instead of focusing on learning what will be required of him for the next four years, instead of focusing on filling his cabinet with qualified appointees, instead of firming up his policies so they make some sort of sense, he's about to embark on a "victory tour." Yes, folks, you read that right - he's about to hold more rallies. Why? He's not campaigning anymore, so rallies are not necessary. You know why, though? Because having a rally is WAY more fun than ACTUALLY DOING YOUR FUCKING JOB!

This is not a man who understands the importance of what he's just been elected to do, nor one who is taking it seriously. This is not a man who wants to serve this nation, to represent the people. No, this a man who wants to rule over it. This is a man who decided he wanted to attain the most important job in this country just to say he could do it. This is a man who sees the position of President as a starring role in his own reality show. This is a man who expects everyone around him to do his bidding while he claims all the accolades. This is a man who only wants people to shower him with praise and thinks criticism is abjectly wrong. This is a man who says what people want to hear while laughing behind their backs at how incredibly naive they are to believe him. This is a man who is only out for himself. This is a man who doesn't give a fuck about the working class who are struggling unless it's to see how much money they can make him. This is a man who will completely and totally fuck over this nation.

I may respect the office of President; but I'm sorry, I cannot respect the man who has been elected to be President.

The Decimation of Democracy

By Robin Lee

In my 43 years on this earth, there are several events which will forever be etched in my memory and have shaped my life in some way – the Challenger Space Shuttle explosion, the death of Kurt Cobain, the Columbine High School shootings, the 9/11 attacks, the Pulse Nightclub shootings, and the 2016 presidential election. The night of November 8, 2016, was the first time I'd ever sobbed at the outcome of an election.

Sure, there had been other elections where I'd been disappointed with who had been elected, but I was never frightened like I was that night. Never before had I felt like our democracy was on the precipice of crumbling. Yet that night, with a single party holding the presidency and a full majority in Congress, with a man who had spread fear, hate and lies being elected to the highest office in our country, I saw the United States dangling on that precipice and I was scared.

Through his campaign and since his election, I've witnessed a man unraveling in 140 characters on Twitter. Since the election, his tweet storms every morning over the most irrelevant issues are showing the world that we are being led by an unhinged man. Already his tweets have increased tensions with China and have offended two of our closest allies – Mexico and Australia – all because he can't control himself. He's so easily upset when anyone is critical of him that he won't let it go for days on end. These are not the traits we need in a leader. His behavior is so erratic that I fear he may trigger an avoidable war.

It is becoming more and more evident to me that DJT doesn't want to be the head of a democratic country; he wants to rule as a monarch or dictator. He's surrounded himself with advisors who are masters of propaganda and spin who seem to want to cement his position as the sole ruler of America. The President proclaims a desire to unify the United States, but every single action he takes or statement he makes seems to be contrary to that aim.

Each cabinet nominee and staff appointee seems to undermine all that he's preached from his bully pulpit. With every Executive Order he's signed since taking office less than three weeks ago, it feels like we are being steered toward the destruction of everything this nation was built upon. Both the President and his closest advisors, I see men and women who appear to have no understanding of and no respect for the Constitution. Even among Congress I see people who are putting the GOP platform and their own interests above the concerns of their constituents.

Part of the reason the DJT's being elected was his appeal to working people, the middle class. They because they felt like he heard their cries for help and recognized their dissatisfaction with career politicians who didn't listen. The irony is that the new President and Congress are still not listening; they keep right on doing whatever the hell they want to.

Evidence of Russian interference in our election is extremely troubling as well. Throughout the campaign DJT insisted the race was rigged. Turns out it was; but even though he won the necessary electoral votes, he still claims it's all rigged because of "millions" of illegal votes. This is another one of his assertions that isn't supported by facts or evidence. Truth is apparently no longer a desired trait for anything with this administration. Unfortunately, the President's penchant for stretching the truth or outright making up his own facts will get the US into some serious and potentially dangerous situations. I waffle between believing they're all just that clueless to them being so cunning as to be downright evil. Either way, our current reality is strange and terrifying.

Aside from the dangerous and dire state of our democracy, the erosion of human decency as a result of DJT's campaign and election is astounding and very sad. The thoughts that many kept under wraps are now freely flowing without regard to how destructive they are. Some are now going out and verbally and, in some cases, physically attacking those who are different than they – i.e. not white, straight and male. Some are invoking the name of the President as their reason that it's "okay" to be a racist, sexist, misogynistic, xenophobic, Islamophobic, homophobic asshole.

Before the election, I didn't think much of walking around my neighborhood after dark; I never felt unsafe.

Now, I worry about being accosted just because DJT's rise has resulted in a sense of entitlement of men over women. The slogan, "Make America Great Again," is a ridiculous fallacy if this is what his presidency is going to take us back to.

Resist

By Robin Lee

Tired
Weary from the bombardment
Exhausted from the battle
And this war is only just beginning
Some days retreat seems the better course
But we can't hide or give up
This fight is much too important
The cornerstone is crumbling
Innocent lives hang in the balance
Our very existence is at risk
There is evil seeping through the fabric
Oozing into the crevices we've refused to acknowledge
It's always been there
Lying dormant under the guise of congeniality
Yet the veil of civility has been shredded
Allowing the villains to surface
We cannot let them overtake us
We will not accept defeat
We must RESIST

qr

About the author:

Snarky Southern lady who likes to wax poetic and sprinkle her prose with a pinch of sugar and a dash of spice. Author of Bittersweet Illusion, a poetry collection, and the upcoming novel Playing Dirty.

Author's website: www.ugly-beautiful.com

Untitled

By Olivia Linden

All we need is love

But first let's work on compassion...

It's a cold world. It always has been. As much as it may seem like we are experiencing trying times, it's really just a phase in the evolution of our society. For many years, certain socioeconomic groups have been incubated in a what I call a bubble. It's where you may see or hear bad things going on in the world, but it has no effect on your life. The climate in our country is ever changing, and the bubbles are bursting. This presidency is going to put us all to the test, and I believe that compassion is what we need to make it through.

The 70's, 80's and 90's were a thriving time for middle and upper middle class America. Now, the middle is being thinned out. The troubles of our country are hitting closer to home. The injustices that haven't been "your" problem are getting harder to ignore. This is a time where sitting on the fence is no longer an option. Hiding behind prejudice is no longer an option.

Are we going to come together and be "Americans" or are we going to continue to let race, ethnicity, gender, sexual orientation, political affiliation, or even sports continue to divide us? Why can't we feel compassion for someone just because we are different? This is what scares me, and what we need to really cultivate. No matter our differences, we are all American and should all have the same rights and freedoms. It's the American way, and we are watching it being snatched away from us and being replaced with ugliness and divisiveness.

Corruption and power have always existed in the fabric of our nation, like a virus. Now the virus is growing out of control. It's being made clear to us how much our voices don't matter to those who are in a position of power to make change. We can't afford to turn on each other. We can't be fooled by the numerous ploys to keep us separated. We need to find the compassion in our hearts, that connection to others. It's the first step to being able to truly love each other, and we need that now more than ever.

qr

About the author:

Olivia Linden was born in New York, but raised in both Queens, NY and San Antonio, TX. As a shy young girl, writing was her creative outlet. Mini plays, short stories, poems and even a few comic strips were created from her love of writing and reading books. She also loves to blog about relationships and social issues when she has the time.

Author's website: http://www.vialinden.com/

The Day Reality Set In

By Harper Miller

On November 8, 2016, I woke up bright eyed and bushy tailed excited to vote. It was going to be a historic day—we'd elect our first woman president! It had been a long time coming, but we were on the path to four more years of greatness. Woo!!!

I usually wake up between 5:00-5:30 AM during the week. My goal is to try and get a workout in before the full-time gig, but that doesn't always go according to plan. That particular morning, I voted and instead of going to the gym, I then walked to the train station, which is about a mile away from where I live (that's about 20 city blocks for those not familiar with the NYC set up) to get my workout in that way.

I strolled into my polling place, my local library, which is about five blocks away from my apartment building. I headed up the stairs and immediately noticed the long line. I checked in with the people sitting at the front thinking, "Damn, this is going to take longer than I intended," despite it being 6:15 in the morning. I was pleasantly surprised when the woman checking off my name informed me that there wasn't a wait for my district. I could go in. SUPER FIST PUMP!

I stepped into the booth, closed the curtain, clicked the little buttons, and watched my selections light up green.

The entire thing took about two minutes tops. No matter what anyone says, voting is an action in which every American should proudly participate. It was a proud moment for me, especially as a woman of color. I am all too familiar with the long, hard battle my ancestors fought to afford me this right. It would be an insult to their legacy for me, or ANY person of color, to sit out an election because of dislike for the candidates. It's an absurd way of thinking. We (and when I say 'we' I'm referring to all Americans) often take our privileges for granted. There are still people who reside in countries where their opinion regarding who heads their government isn't counted. Never forget this.

As I exited the library, a woman sitting inside her truck with her arm hanging out of the driver's side window called out to me, "That was fast. Hope you voted Trump!"

I had no idea my movements were being tracked. That aside, my first inclination was to say, "Are you kidding me?" But I bit my tongue and replied in a lighthearted manner. "It was an easy vote."

She smiled and went back to talking to the man standing near her truck. I drowned them out as I walked away, but I could faintly hear them say, "He's what this country needs."

For fuck's sake.

I went to work and was giddy for the remainder of the day. My Facebook feed was flooded with people posting their "I voted" stickers. I made a post on Facebook declaring my unwavering support for HRC despite having issues with her. I put aside my personal feelings and voted for the greater good. When I stepped into the voting booth, I was thinking of what she could do for the entire country as opposed to special interest groups and lobbyists. I thought about the example I wanted to set for our children. I thought about how much progress had been made in the last eight years and who would be the best fit to keep our country stable and represent us in international affairs. I voted for the person who best represented themselves on the campaign trail. It had been a shitty couple of months, but one camp didn't negate facts and didn't act like an overgrown manchild during the debates.

I jokingly posted on my non-author Facebook account that I was heading to the liquor store on my way home from work to pick up a bottle of wine. I'd need it if the election went in a different direction. A few months earlier, I had also posted on my non-author account about how likely it would be for DT to win the election based on a Michael Moore post I read. My friends flipped out.

The comments could be summed up as the following: WHAT ARE YOU POSTING? STOP IT WITH THE SCARE TACTICS. THAT WOULD NEVER HAPPEN!

It happened.

I had my glass of wine, and around 9:30 PM I tuned to PBS to watch the election results come in. By 11, I had finished the bottle.

Goddamn electoral college.

I couldn't believe it was looking like DT would win the presidency. HRC was so far behind in electoral votes. Upon deeper reflection, it shouldn't have been a surprise to me that the early returns were from states that were pro-DT and also part of the Confederacy. There's a correlation between a candidate who runs on a platform with blatant racism. Equating black and brown people as uneducated, rapists, and terrorists living in squalor, and the overwhelming support in a part of our nation that longs for the "good ole days."

Then, of course, there's the number done on the Voting Rights Act through voter suppression. When you can't win by legitimate means, suppress the citizens!

We had a good run, democracy.

I went to bed hoping it was all some bad dream. I woke up at 5:30 the following morning and immediately turned on the news. It wasn't a bad dream. DT was the president-elect of the United States. Michael Moore was right.

I couldn't get out of bed. I lay in a fetal position, crying. Needless to say, I didn't go to work that day. I kept trying to wrap my head around how people could be so naive. Then, demographic breakdowns according to race were released, and 94% of black women voted for Hillary Clinton and 53% of white women voted for DT. These were the most startling demographic breakdowns for me. I had to let those results marinate for a bit. I never understood how people could vote against their best interests, but it's a pattern repeated throughout history. Individuals value race over social issues.

Despite the fact that we'd had eight years of a Black president and a Black family in the White House, it was clear people had had enough. The "liberal" idea of unity and making America a better place for all citizens was not to happen. We were to regress to the "good ole days."

I think the most troubling thing for me in the aftermath of the election is, as I write this, we're two weeks into this administration, and people continue to say, "Give him a chance!"

Based on all the choices he's made with his cabinet, his nominees to head government agencies, and his executive orders that didn't go through the proper vetting and alienated a sect of our population due to religious affiliation…HOW MANY MORE CHANCES ARE WE TO GIVE?

He's not a goddamn cat. He doesn't get nine lives. The man has made a laundry list of questionable decisions and statements pre- and post- election, and yet we're still to give him a chance? There has not been a single clear statement or action to unify this country. He has continued to spew divisive and nonsensical drivel.

One thing that constantly nags at me are the parents who voted for him.

How do you look your child in the eye and tell them that bullying is wrong? They come home from school saying they're being picked on by classmates for any given reason. How do you tell your child that what's happening to them is wrong? How can you say it with a straight face?

How do you tell your daughter that she's entitled to respect? That no one has the right to violate her, but you found it acceptable to vote for a man accused of multiple sexual assaults (including the rape of his ex-wife)?

How do you tell your child who lives with a disability that there's nothing wrong with them? That they are loved no matter what despite the fact that you voted for a man who openly mocked a disable reporter, and who has not once ever apologized for his offensive actions?

Lastly, how do you tell your child that they should strive to be unique? How do you convey to them the idea that people are special, but you voted for a man who thinks Mexicans are rapists, although there might be *some* good ones, *all* Muslims are terrorists, *all* Blacks live in inner city impoverished war zones and have little to no education? You supported a man whose Vice President thinks LGBTIQA people are an abomination and conversion therapy is what they need.

What do you say to your child who is a part of the LGBTIQA community? How can you tell them you support them but you voted for an administration who doesn't fully support their existence?

My guess is many parents who voted for this ticket tell

themselves whatever they have to so that they're able to sleep at night. The sad part is you'll have to justify it when your child inevitably gets suspended from school for sexually assaulting a fellow student in the restroom.

Their reasoning? "Well our President did it, why can't I?"

We lead by example, and the example you've held up as a beacon of hope is going to set this country back decades. Hope you're ready for the bumpy ride.

Me? I'm part of the sect of Americans who refuses to normalize hateful rhetoric and behavior. I have my work cut out for me for the next four years, but I'm in it to win it.

We all deserve for our civil rights to be upheld, and for me, there is no debating that topic.

qr

About the Author:

Harper Miller is a thirty-something native New Yorker. She's traveled the world and lived in a variety of places but always finds her way back to the Big Apple. A lackluster love life leaves time to explore new interests; for Harper it is writing. *The Sweetest Taboo: An Unconventional Romance* is her debut novel. In her mind, the perfect Alpha male possesses intellect, humor, and a kinky streak that rivals the size of California.

When she isn't writing, Harper utilizes her graduate degree in the field of medical research. She enjoys fitness-related activities, drinking copious amounts of wine, and going on bad dates.

Author's website: www.authorharpermiller.com

Jackson 2.0

By G. Miller

When Mitch McConnell called Andrew Jackson a "voice of the people," and then compared him to Donald Trump, I knew what time it was, but it wasn't like I didn't suspect it before. All the signs were there. Trump called Mexicans rapists. He supported stop and frisk. He insisted the Central Park Five were guilty. These are points that I've repeated over and over until I knew them by heart because I couldn't allow myself to forget who was running for president.

Trump's supporters would always question whether he was racist. They would say liberals were just attacking him and the media was twisting his words. They would call anyone who disagreed with Trump "snowflakes" or "libtards" and still do. I'll admit that I was convinced he was a bigot, but there was a slim chance that he was misunderstood. Very slim.

But then the Jackson comparisons came and it became clear. Trump said he was giving the country back to "the people" during his inauguration address. Steve Bannon compared that speech to Jackson too. Here's the thing though. Jackson was not the voice for all people. He was the voice for white people. Jackson didn't represent black people or natives when he ordered the Negro Fort Massacre. He didn't represent natives when he signed the Indian Removal Act that started the "Trail of Tears." Anyone who thinks Trump represents "the people" while comparing him to Jackson either doesn't understand what they're saying or believes in the kind of white nationalism that Jackson acted upon when he slaughtered people escaping an oppressive nation or forcefully removed a tribe from their own land for the sake of white supremacy.

Trump, according to his own supporters, is comparable to a genocidal president who targeted political refugees and native tribes, and that's supposed to be a compliment. Our new president didn't own an endorsement from the Ku Klux Klan, but he hasn't backed away from this comparison, and that should alarm any American who believes in living a life of goodwill.

Jackson is a white nationalist's American hero, and Trump hung his portrait in the Oval Office before seeking to build a wall between us and Mexico while demanding the Mexican government pay for it. He hung a portrait of Jackson in the Oval Office before instituting a ban from seven countries because they are majority Muslim. So far his presidency would make Jackson proud. He's fighting to preserve white identity like he would've wanted by keeping as many brown people out as possible. It's only a matter of time before he finds a way to hit black people next. Our freedom and fight for equality has born a thorn in white supremacy's side for generations.

If you're a Trump supporter, and you're reading this, I have to ask if you actually want a Jackson 2.0. Do you want a modern "Trail of Tears"? Well, something tells me Trump's immigration policy will satisfy you.

Would you like a millennial Negro Fort Massacre? Well, just wait until Trump gets around to sending the feds to Chicago because, really, he won't be sending them to stop and frisk white people. That's not the Jacksonian way of doing things. Trump supporters, are you really willing to subject America's people of color to another Jackson? If you are, don't complain when people call you racist. You just contributed to handing the Oval Office to an ideology of racial oppression for monetary gain, and it speaks volumes about the state of our nation when the morals of its people can be bought by extremists.

qr

About the author:

G.Miller is a journalist and fiction writer from Connecticut who writes about sports, race, and culture. He has written four novels and contributed to sports and politics stories for USA Today and OZY.

Author's website: www.noapologiesnation.com

Mourning America

by Morgan Jane Mitchell

I didn't cry on election night. I turned off the news, poured a glass of wine and smoked five cigarettes on the front porch by myself—for real, but don't worry, I've since quit. I went to bed, hoping it was all an error. It had to be. There was no way hate could win. Lying in bed that night, I actually thought for a moment that maybe I'd died and gone to Hell. The next day, I stayed away from all media and didn't even check who won. Before long my son texted me from school, saying, "America is dead."

Raised in Inez, Kentucky, where LBJ started the war on poverty, aka eastern Kentucky or coal country, in part by my grandmother who'd pulled herself out of extreme poverty to become an entrepreneur I spent more time than I can quantify sitting in her restaurant listening to folks talk politics. Having heard it all, from my grandmother, a Democrat and the liberal teachers, miners and preachers and from Republicans like my father, the conservative business owners, Sunday school teachers and farmers, my political leanings were formed early. In my mind these were all good, respectable people with different opinions, even the teacher who scolded me in the fifth grade for calling Dan Quayle stupid. Therefore, when someone says they were raised to think it impolite to talk politics, frankly, I don't give a damn.

When Hillary announced she would run again, I cried tears of joy. This thirty-eight-year-old, mother of three, a romance author and lifelong Democrat had more enthusiasm than I knew what to do with, despite the claims otherwise. Then the primaries got ugly, like they often do.

Hillary's crushing 2008 loss had previously taken a toll on many of her supporters. I wasn't sure I could go through it again. Back then, yes, we are going back. History is important, now more than ever, so bear with me. Hillary's supporters, Democrats, who'd been defenders of civil and human rights felt painted as mere racists for wanting the more experienced candidate—it hurt! We wanted Universal Healthcare not the ACA. We wanted more gun control and less ties to Wall Street. We were proud our candidate had marched in a gay pride parade when Obama had not at the time, all petty differences now. I became a PUMA, which stood for "Party Unity, My Ass". We fought on to the convention and threatened to not support Obama in the general election. After all, John McCain was no G.W. Bush. Nevertheless, when Hillary wholeheartedly endorsed Barack Obama, most of us fell in line.

I'm ashamed to say that it took me a while, but I ended up supporting Obama. I'm glad I did.

Why rehash this now?

Because this was where Donald came in. Though always gross, in 2008 he was a registered Democrat and an obvious Clinton Supporter in the Democratic primary—in my memory, a PUMA if there ever was one, publicly refusing to support Obama in the general election because Hillary wasn't on the ticket. It was like Donald never woke from 2008's primary craze. He registered as a Republican in 2009 and ingested a steady diet of what we now call fake news. Unfortunately, PUMA or not, he'd taken the bait left for them. He'd been fooled by the right-wing lie that Obama hadn't been born in the United States, amongst other things. Even back then misinformation was only a quick search away. Looking for validation that my candidate was the best choice, I'd almost been taken in myself.

While I gave up politics and turned to writing fiction, Donald ended up using his name and platform to demand to see Obama's long form birth certificate and defend conspiracy theories on CNN's Larry King Live, the View, You Tube and then Facebook for years before running for President. I wasn't the only one who remembered Donald's support of Hillary. At the beginning of his campaign, confused, some claimed Donald's candidacy was a false flag to give Hillary the election.

Consequently, during this 2016 election, this not being my first or second rodeo, I could relate to the Bernie or Bust movement and the third-party voters. After all, in college, I'd signed a petition to get Ralph Nader on the ballot that regrettably ended up helping bring about G.W. Bush's defeat of Al Gore in 2000. See, I had a couple of lessons learned under my belt that may have enlightened a first-time voter or reasoned with a protest voter. I wanted to tell them they were being fooled, not by Bernie, Jill or Gary but by politics itself and this time with the help of memes, bots on Twitter and the fake news popping up right in their Facebook feed, they didn't even need to search it out—not to mention the false equivalence and sexism on steroids.

Donald's campaign had not been a Republican or populist revolution but one of revulsion. I witnessed otherwise sensible people become paranoid and filled with hate to support him. However, every time I tried to speak out, I was bombarded with horrifying comments from the left and right. Too quickly, I decided that I couldn't change anyone's mind online and didn't need the headache. Instead, I quietly volunteered, donated and went to rallies. I got my Hillary selfie, something that didn't exist in 2008, but kept politics off my social media for the most part. Besides, there was no way we could lose to someone like Donald Trump, right? Like millions (yes, millions) of other like-minded people, people who didn't want the drama, I hid and found support in secret Facebook groups.

Big mistake!

Still, I didn't cry when we lost. I was too angry, too suspicious. I was too hurt for my children who I'd raised to be compassionate Americans, to accept people of every gender, race, nationality, ability, religion or sexual orientation, who I'd imparted the importance of religious freedom and generosity, who I'd encouraged to become free thinkers and educate themselves. They had to deal with the fact that the bullies at their school who flew confederate flags, slapped "Trump that Bitch" bumper stickers on their pickups, shouted out like brainwashed zombies, "Build the wall," during any discussion of Mexico, chanted, "Lock her up," at any mention of Secretary Clinton and told foreign looking students that they'd be deported as soon as Trump won, had just won, as well.

Hate had won.

I listened to Hillary's concession speech and felt like crying, but crying would make it real. I looked to our leaders and voices on the left for help. I wanted them to audit the vote, to recount the swing states we lost by a tiny margin, just the margin Donald needed to win. Hillary's popular vote totals kept rolling in, growing to the levels the polls predicted. Many voices rose up asking for an audit only to be squashed by those on the left that had warned us that Hillary wouldn't win in the first place and by some who declared a revolution would be better, that Donald and Hillary were the same anyway.

How could some who were telling us how bad it was likely to get also tell us that they wouldn't call for an audit? Had they been crying wolf about Donald? Or did they just happen to be the ones who stood to gain the most from being the opposition, from a revolution. I couldn't believe, during the initial protests, some were still saying, give Donald Trump a chance. (Even just the other day—I'm looking at you Dennis Kucinich, who may or may not have been body snatched.)

Yes, Hillary had asked us to give Donald a chance during her concession speech, too, but what could she really say? She had warned us. She tried her best and then went for a walk in the woods. Most of us wanted to join her.

So many on both sides had warned us. What we wouldn't give to have Jeb! a freaking Bush, exclamation point and all.

Jill Stein took up the charge for the recounts and in our desperation, many of us forgot that she campaigned against us and had a mysterious lunch with Putin and General Flynn. I had hope that Jill was as devastated as the rest of us and wanted to do something noble. We gave Jill millions only for the recount efforts to be squashed by lawsuit after lawsuit.

Come to find out almost three million more people voted for Hillary than Donald, but he won where it counted, where there was more land than people. Still the media, left and right, tried to analyze why we lost although we had won more votes. Russian meddling was swept under the rug despite calls for investigations from respected Republicans. Donald tried to erase our majority with "alternative facts" of vast voter fraud.

After the "Sad.", poorly attended inauguration, we marched. I took my sister and marched in Lexington, Kentucky, wishing I didn't know that the Women's March left Hillary's name off the honorees' list on purpose and wouldn't add it, despite our calls to do so. The good news, my sister who had never protested before felt inspired. As I wore my old 2008, brown and turquoise Hillary shirt, and witnessed 5000 or more people in my red state of all skin tones, old and young, in wheelchairs, in heels, in drag, some with pink hair, others with their heads covered, male and female veterans, mothers with babies strapped to them, fathers with babies strapped to them, the dogs, the children, I wanted to feel inspired. It was a beautiful, moving day, but I still felt erased.

No, the march hadn't been about one woman or just about women. But leaving Clinton's name off the list of revolutionary leaders who paved the way for the march while using her quote, "Women's rights are human rights and human rights are women's rights," was a slap in the face to some who have always fought this battle, just another way to say we weren't enthusiastic or authentic enough. To go away so the others can play. Again, even though we won more votes, it just hadn't been enough. What was worse, we were still fighting each other.

Again, I didn't cry.

Then Donald's Executive Order on Immigration came on a Friday night—you know, the Muslim Ban he campaigned on but then also walked back during the election. Protests were happening all over, in and out of airports. When I watched an Iranian mother finally reunited with her five-year-old son who'd been detained for hours, I lost it.

I finally cried.

This was no longer the America I knew and loved. America had died, just like my son had texted the day after the election.

Yes, this is all real. Yes, all the crazy Donald spouted during the election, that even most rational Republicans went on the record to call out, is real. Donald wasn't just using divisive rhetoric to win over the masses, like some speculated. Yes, instead of affordable college, clean energy and the like, we'll get deregulating everything, all get cancer and a #fuckingwall, and that's just the beginning. Believe me, we'll pay for it all, bigly. And no, you aren't imagining the signs of fascism here and around the world.

Who will save us?

Up until this point I believed myself when I told my kids that, yes, things might suck for a couple of years, but there are sensible Republicans in the majority who are great, wonderful, tremendous people (to use Donald's few words) who would never let the worst happen. However, these executive orders and cabinet appointments have shaken that assumption and not just the confirmation of Betsy DeVos. To think our elected officials have to ask for our calls and emails to help them decide how to vote? Really?

A Republican or two might make a statement in opposition, but they soon fall in line, ready to pass whatever they can while they can. It seems like the Democrats have been playing like Hillary in the debates, just letting Donald do his thing and America see how crazy he gets. We get it. Please stop. We want you to fight back.

Therefore, I say our fate cannot be placed in the hands of our elected officials or in the hands of the leaders of any resistance. Remember, some resisting now said that they wanted this, that a revolution would be better than protecting our rights. Remember, for some, this is the long game, a book deal or campaign run down the line. I say this and all I've said not to fight but to inform.

We must all lead. We must take up the fight for what we know is right ourselves. We must stay informed and inform others. We must not let our petty differences allow hate to prevail. We must not erase even one of us to appease the masses. We must not do any of this blindly or quietly. We must not always be polite or go high. We must bear witness where our friends and family can see what we stand for and against.

Yes, we must post on social media as much as we hate to—God help us all.

qr

About the author:

Bestselling erotic romance and paranormal author, Morgan Jane Mitchell spent years blogging politics and health trends before she rediscovered her love of writing fiction. Trading politicians for bloodsuckers of another kind, she's now the author of bestselling post-apocalyptic fantasy novel, Sanguis City.

Author's website: www.themorganjane.com

I fear

By Katherine Rhodes

The breathing is soft and shallow.
I am still glad to hear it, though
occasionally
it grows to a rattling snore.

The laughter in the driven snow
is bold, innocent, joyous
though
a bit jarring when they grow close.

I stand in the place
where Liberty was born
Where the words were written
where our freedom began
and
a sheen of frightened tears
blurs the scene, dims the light

I fear
I will never feel the swell of
pride

I fear
I will never know the joy of
patriotism

Standing. Wondering.
Is there hope
Is there joy
Is there any chance
that I will not fear again?

I fear
the breathing will cease for want
of care

I fear
the laughter will go silent for fear
of authority

I fear
that I will never see
what I once knew
as a child.

I fear
that my child will never see
what we could be

I fear
US.

qr

About the author:

A lackadaisical laundry goddess, and an expert in the profundities of bad music and awful literature-thanks to her husband-Katherine strives to find balance in the universe and time to cook dinner.

Author's website: www.Katherinerhodes.com

Letter to Mr. President

By C. Ricketts

President Donald Trump
The White House
1600 Pennsylvania Avenue NW
Washington, DC 20500.

January 31st, 2017

Dear President Trump,

I'd like to tell you about my daughter, Nikki. She is a vibrant, 25-year old rascal who loves to dance and without judgment, grabs anyone's hand to dance with her. She is a funny goofball whose laugh is contagious and exudes joy for all (sometimes for no identifiable reason at all). She is developmentally and physically challenged with a genetic defect called Holoprosencephaly (HPE, once known as arhinencephaly). It is a cephalic disorder in which the prosencephalon (the forebrain of the embryo) fails to develop into two hemispheres. She has a secondary challenge called Diabetes insipidus, a rare disorder that occurs when a person's kidneys pass an abnormally large volume of urine. In short, she is non-verbal, incontinent, and has the mental development of a 1 year-old.

These challenges are often met with glances of pity,

stares of offense, gaping mouths of disgust, and an onslaught of prejudice. However, I see them as God's testimony to his faith in my ability to rise above that and share Nikki's joy and unconditional love and acceptance with the world. When people stare, I invite them to ask questions and meet her—to experience her happiness in any environment.

I am not a practicing Catholic, yet I still do believe in God. His acceptance of me despite my faults, my mistakes, and my politics is evident because he gave Nikki to me as a gift. She has been (and continues to be) my teacher. Patience, tolerance for those that do not understand my point of view, unconditional love, acceptance, and overall, how to be a better person. She is the epitome of what humanity should be. She hates no one, judges no one or let other's judgment of her steal her joy. She is precocious and funny, finding the tiniest things hilarious.

The purpose of my letter is not to push any of my positions to sway you on your current path, with the exception of one. The most important one. Support Humanity, not spur the divide.

That cannot be done through hate, rushed actions, and hasty emotionally charged reactions.

You have the ability to calm our great nation, that is in extreme turmoil, yet you allowed your Press Secretary, Sean Spicer to take the horrific tragedy of the Quebec Mosque shootings and bring up your Immigration Ban. He used one of the most heart-wrenching attacks on Canadian soil to advocate your Executive Order signed on Friday when it was **unconfirmed** if the shooter was a legal/illegal Muslim visitor/immigrant.

This misleading tactic is deplorable. ESPECIALLY in light of this past weekend's reactions to your Executive Order. Emotions are already running hot and fast. Judgments are flaring hatred on both sides of the argument. People are acting on their reaction before accurate facts are reported. We are becoming a nation entirely embroiled in politics when they have never been active before. I am included in that·statistic.

Mr. Spicer could have made some diplomatic attempt to calm the nation at least on your behalf. To relay verified facts so that each side of the divide could be informed with accurate reporting. **SIX** hours prior to the press conference, reports were coming in stating the arrest of Alexandre Bissonnette, a native French-Canadian, that worked in the civil service for the Quebec government, was the sole shooter. Mr. Spicer's press conference was held a 1:30 EST. The **FOUR** hours in between was surely enough time to get vetted facts about the suspect and use a rational mind to address the press accordingly. This man speaks on your behalf so to that I say, how dare you use this random act of **HOME-GROWN** terror to ignite more outage. How dare you use the senseless killing of SIX law-abiding citizens doing nothing but honoring their faith, to support your agenda. In error, I might add.

Honestly, I fear for my daughter's Medicaid and Social Security Disability benefits. I fear for what will happen to her if anything happens to me. But what I fear the most, down to the fiber of my being, is the hate that is being inspired by your current inactions. Hate knows no color or boundaries. When you allow one form of hate to grow, you allow all of them. By your silence, you are condoning your citizens to act on ANY kind of hate. You are allowing the hate to fester and that is dangerous.

It has been documented throughout history as the instigator of mass destructions of nations and war. Hate for your fellow man because of the color of their skin, the God they pray to, their beliefs and opinions, the way they look, their disabilities and differences. We are all God's children and in my eyes, God doesn't make mistakes.

As the Commander-In-Chief of my beloved United States of America, it is your responsibility to protect all of your employers, ie: we the people. It is your duty to sooth the tensions with words that will bring us ALL hope. Hope that the next four years won't be like the last eleven days.

Thank you for your time reading this longer than intended letter,

C. Ricketts

A Disenchanted Citizen

qr

About the author:

Indie Author of romance, but love my insanely suspenseful romances the best. Mother, wife, reader & I knit, but not at the same time. Mentally writing my life story, but it's an organic work of art so remains incomplete.

Author's website: www.smexyindieauthor.com

Look at us

By Kimberly Rose

Look at us.

Take off the clothes.

The pressed and ironed

The tattered and torn.

Take off the headdresses

The wraps

The name brands.

Wash away the makeup

The frown lines

The pigment of skin

Set down the accounts

The pennies

The income

The debts

Set aside the rule books

The doctrines

The scriptures of faith.

Look at us.

Look at all of us.

We are all hearts made of the same blood

Beating in chests made of the same bone.

We are all the breath of the same lungs

Breathing into the same air.

We are all souls searching for the same meanings to
satisfy the same desires.

We all fear and falter

Break, fall, and fail,

Beat with pride

Bleed out humility

We all reach and rise

Trust, hope, and love

Soften with trust

Reach for respect

Look at us.

We hate.

Judge, ban, segregate

Box ourselves in, and pile ourselves up until we topple

Too heavy from the weight of our fears.

Fears that make us hate, ban, judge segregate.

Fear of what's unfamiliar

What's misunderstood

Fear of the unforeseen

Look at us.

We're failing.

To teach love.

To give love.

To be love.

When under it all,

The unfamiliar, the misunderstood,

The uncertain, the unexpected....

There's a heart.

A heart in a chest made of mountains and plains, deserts and forests

With breath expanding from ocean to ocean inhaling dreams and exhaling promise.

With bones built upon

Sacrifice.

Triumph.

Strength.

Look at us.

Look at all of us.

qr

About the author:

Kimberly Rose lives on the island of Oahu for now, until her husband's career in the Navy moves them again. A lover of the written word she enjoys reading, writing, and teaching Language Arts.

Author's website:
www.authorkimberlyrose.wordpress.com

Paranoia

By Amalie Silver

I've felt for a while now that the Right's agenda is to get people to "see the light," so to speak. And that most of the things they believe are good for our government and country are faith-based.

I didn't understand their frustration until a few months ago, to be honest. It wasn't until my husband explained it to me that I got a sense of how unfair things had gotten for them: policies they don't agree with have been shoved in their faces. Bitter pills to swallow when the Bible and its teachings have implied that these things do *not* align with their moral compasses.

Christians--and most religions--are all about doing good things for people. Loving thy neighbor and all that. I was raised a Lutheran, baptized and all. I spent many summers and fall retreats at a Christian camp in central Minnesota. They're good people with good moral compasses. They're kind and loving, they give a helping hand when needed, and many of them are educated and intelligent people.

This has never been about which side boasts the higher IQ. It has never been about email servers or pussy-grabbing or Benghazi or Muslims.

It's about our paranoia.

Luckily, I'm medicated enough for my own anxiety to be able to put this into words today.

When I was growing up in my medium-sized city just south of St. Paul, Minnesota, my father sustained a home, two cars, a wife, two daughters, and a cat or two on a $35,000 per year as a Federal Express (FedEx) delivery driver. In the 1980s, our neighborhood was a safe place to be. I rode my bike as often as I fell off it. At the age of eight, I could walk a mile to the nearest Burger King with my friends just to get some fries and a shake without fear that I'd get kidnapped or raped. Even in high school, major crime was rare. The biggest safety hazard was high school kids drinking, driving, and listening to Korn.

But things have become…complicated.

We all remember what we were doing on September 11, 2001, when we heard about the first plane. We were tough, though. Americans banded together and formed a united front against the attackers. Our presidents did their jobs as best as they could with the information they had. And we haven't had another attack of its magnitude since.

But there's one thing that happens on 9/11 every year, and it couldn't be more fitting. It's the hashtag that circulates on social media: #neverforget.

We haven't. In fact, it's part of a long list of worries we have for ourselves and our children.

And it has festered.

With the rise in internet and social media over the past twenty years, some of the most horrifying and sadistic crimes in the world have made their way into our views. From rape and mutilation to child molestation and children bleeding in foreign countries, those images are things we never forget. We never saw these kinds of things, this often, on the nightly news in the 80s. Hell, we barely saw them in the 90s. If we did, it wasn't half of the information we get about them now. Those stories were reserved for the two-minute segment Channel Five spotlighted between weather and traffic.

We have so much damn information these days that it has gotten to the point that we don't truly know what is real and what is fake. Broadcasters have always been concerned about ratings, but they really started digging deep when social media became the new chosen favorite for news. The news channels' quests became more about what would get them clicks than what was factual. The more absurd and horrifying the headline, the more people would tune in to what they had to say.

And so that is when our *extreme* paranoia began.

The whole damn country has PTSD from seeing the things we have on network news and our newsfeeds. The horrifying stories that you can't unsee plague your psyche and seep into your memory, never to escape. Perhaps these kinds of stories were there all along, but we just didn't have the blood-seeking journalists finding them. Or maybe there were some things that were too gruesome to put on Channel Five at six o'clock. Whatever the case, I would wager money on the fact that the crimes and horrid stories we've heard in the past twenty years had *always* been happening. We either filtered them out or we didn't know about them.

#neverforget

We won't. We couldn't even if we wanted to.

And now we have Trump and his administration blaming America's crime on a handful of countries in the Middle East. Oh, and Mexico. Yes, I'm sure there are a few immigrants that commit crimes. Perhaps even violent crimes. But you can't convince me that they're doing more to us than we're doing to ourselves. You would've had a shot convincing me before the 2016 election, but seeing the hate and violence that's out there right now proves that we have enough problems of our own. Sorry, but there's a whole lot of shit being spewed from both directions right now, and we've found ourselves in the midst of a civil war. Banning a handful of Syrian refugees and building a wall along the southern border certainly aren't going to fix what's going on in our own closets, folks. Quite a few demons have tumbled out, and they don't speak any other language besides English.

We have become a society obsessed with our own paranoia. Sure, we continue to live our lives as best as we can, seeing friends at Starbucks on weekends and tuning into Facebook every night. We keep up the facades that our lives are complete with white picket fences and Tuesday trips to take the twins to dance classes. Adorable pictures, by the way. But I've seen it firsthand. I live in the same house in the same city in the same state that I did in the 1980s. I bought my parents' house. This street used to be bustling with activity on the weekends: kids on bikes, dads out watering their lawns, dogs off leashes, the ice cream man, and small groups taking brisk jogs once or twice around the block.

I see squirrels now. Just squirrels. We even have an eagle that nests in a high oak across the street. For the most part, it's silent.

The older kids that sporadically appear are always looking over their shoulders, walking quickly to their destinations.

Numb. Both sides have become so blinded by fear that they'll do anything to unsee the things they have.

It's almost as if every moral compass in the country has suddenly shut down. No rules apply anymore. All bets are off. Even Christians are bending their rules to fit their political agenda because of fear. Maybe some would argue that's *all* the Republicans ever did. But I believe that faith was designed to bring the best out in a person. The *person*, not the masses. I'm just not convinced that religion has a place in our government, other than a general moral compass. Be kind. Be civilized. Do good. Lend a helping hand. Be faithful, sincere, and passionate.

Fabricated lies. Stretched truths. Christian extremists. Backwoods thinking. At what point did we think this would better our society? At what point do we stop and ask ourselves what is important? Where is our passion for logic, level-headedness, and truth? Half the country thinks "conservative" is a dirty word. And the other half believes the same about the word "liberal." What happened to loving thy neighbor? What happened to respect? Dignity? Kindness?

My advice:

Liberals: Give some folks a break while they adjust to new politically correct language and thought processes. Not everyone loves change the way you do.

Republicans: Don't shun things you don't understand. Enlightenment is man's natural progression and God's will. No matter if your neighbor believes in Him or not, God will still exist.

Libertarians: Keep doing what you do and giving a voice to sanity. This world is desperate for it.

I don't know if I have a solution. But I know one thing: my moral compass is strong and resilient. I will always, under any circumstances, continue looking for the good in people before I seek out the bad. I will continue to love my neighbor, look for the truth, and be a better person than I was yesterday. I will not force my ideals onto someone who isn't ready to hear them, not for the sake of peace-keeping, but for the sake of paranoia. That paranoia is the only common ground all of us share.

My final words: **Grow up. We are America. Let's start acting like it.**

Your Son

By Amalie Silver

If your son was born with purple hair, would you love him any less?

You'd probably say to yourself, "How is that possible?" The doctors would be left scratching their heads, and they would ask you a million questions about your pregnancy.

"Were you taking any medications?"

"Did you have any odd cravings?"

"Did he move around like a *normal* baby would?"

"Did you drink, do drugs, or engage in any risky behavior?"

After scouring the medical charts, they'd hand him over and say, "Congratulations, you have a purple-haired son."

You and your partner would take your son home from the hospital, continue to feed him, change his diapers, coddle him, swaddle him, and love him despite his hair color. In fact, you would barely notice it past the chubby cheeks, the first smiles, the coos, the crawling—and you would dismiss the milestones he didn't hit because you refused to believe he was different.

You'd avoid posting pictures on social media because

you didn't want the questions.

"Why is his hair purple? Did you dye it?"

"Your boy is…strange. What's wrong with him?"

"I'm pretty sure that isn't *normal*. Have you brought him to the doctor?"

You're better off not bringing attention to it. You skip family reunions, play dates, and birthday parties to avoid the questions and strange looks. If you must go, you make sure his hat is secured in place.

You think it's silly. After all, it's just the color of his hair. His hair doesn't define who he is.

He's a *normal* baby.

He's yours.

You love him.

But as time goes on, more people begin to notice the boy with the purple hair. He's walking now, and you want to bring him to early childhood classes so that he can grow up like a *normal* person. You want to do all the things for your child that you would with a brown-haired child.

But this only causes more problems.

The teachers whisper. The boys and girls in class avoid him. You soon realize that no matter how hard you try, no one is going to treat your son the same, because he's *different.*

Still, you persist. You try to get him to engage the other children. You make a plea with your friends for them to accept your purple-haired boy and to let their child play with yours. You can't understand why no one is willing to understand that it's just a minor difference.

Soon, the teachers have decided that he needs to be separated from his peers. What's best for him is to be with other purple-haired boys and girls. They make a recommendation for him to attend a different school, one that specializes in children who aren't *normal.*

They tell you that purple-haired children tend to have specific needs that they can't tend to there. There will be delayed communication, fine motor skills, gross motor skills, and behavioral issues they'll need to address. He'll need more one-on-one help.

Ridiculous! Who are they to tell you that your child isn't perfect? And *normal?*

You read their summation of your boy and it drives a knife through your heart. They're right: he can't stack blocks. He isn't speaking. He's quite clumsy. He lines up cars and marbles into straight lines across the kitchen.

You're not sure what to do, but you think that the teachers must know more than you do about this kind of thing. They must see children with purple hair all the time. So you submit.

Because you love him.

You put him on a bus when he's just twenty months old. His little legs can't even climb up the tall steps to get in, so they carry him. You wave goodbye to your boy, wondering how all of this happened and whether you're doing the right thing.

Four years pass. You've had another baby, you've gotten used to your routine, and your son has new friends. Some have purple hair. Others have orange. One even has blue hair. And your son is happy. He rushes home from school every day to tell you about his friends and the things he learned. He has advanced in academics, specifically mathematics and reading. His teachers all adore him, and his friends can't wait to talk with him about Minecraft.

The special program for purple-haired children has taken your boy and made him a little man. His hair has faded, and it looks much more brown than ever before. You realize that there's no way you could've done it by yourself because you were blinded by your love for him.

You wouldn't have been able to teach him how to stack blocks, because you had tried for months.

You wouldn't have been able to dissuade him from lining up toys in the kitchen, because you didn't realize it was abnormal.

You wouldn't have been able to teach him how to speak, because you didn't understand the way his mind worked.

You want to thank the school district for helping you when you didn't know you needed it...and still do. You want to thank the teachers, the occupational therapists, the speech therapists, and the paras for how hard they worked and advocated for your son.

You hate to admit that they understood him when you couldn't, but you couldn't be more grateful.

And then one day you find out that America hired a Secretary of Education who doesn't believe the program is helping. The Secretary of Education doesn't think the program should exist, let alone have the kind of federal funding it does. The Secretary of Education thinks that America should profit monetarily from education, not academically.

And suddenly your entire world is ripped apart, along with millions of other Americans. You can't understand why your country would think that this program is failing when it has taken their requirements of education for brown-haired children and applied it to your purple-haired child.

They made him as *normal* as he can be by their standards. And now their standards are going to be motivated by profit.

Over 500,000 students in the United States diagnosed with an autism spectrum disorder are enrolled in special education.

Over 400,000 students diagnosed with developmental delays.

350,000 with emotional disturbances.

425,000 with intellectual disabilities.

1,000,000 with speech impairments.

28,000 with visual impairments.

26,000 with traumatic brain injuries.

All served through public school special education programs.

When America says only rich, brown-haired children are allowed schooling, what will we do about the rest of them? Put them out on the streets? Cage them? Tell them, "Sorry, kid, you're not worthy of an education. Seems your potential doesn't meet our standards, but thanks for applying"?

(Statistics taken from nces.ed.gov)

qr

About the author:

Amalie Silver resides in Minnesota with her husband, two toddlers, and black cat, Mr. Fish. She consumes approximately three pots of coffee a day, and credits this for her survival over the past decade.

Author's website: https://amaliesilver.wordpress.com/

I Want to be Wrong

By M. Stratton

I have never wanted to be so wrong in my life as I do now.

I watched and prayed on November eighth that was I was seeing was wrong. I prayed that when I woke up in the morning, it would all have been a dream.

It wasn't.

Every day since November ninth I wake up with my stomach in knots. Every day I pray for peace and acceptance. For love instead of hate. I pray for a better future than the one I see coming, rushing towards us.

I've listened as we've been called whining babies, told to get over it, stop overreacting, you're paranoid, everything is going to be great again.

But it isn't.

It isn't great at all.

On the one hand, I've seen people come together in the millions to march peacefully for a change. It was so beautifully moving and inspiring. People started thinking of others instead of themselves. People came together to show the world the injustices going on here and that there were Americans that cared about the rest of the world. We are all connected to each other in this world. We accept that and embrace the differences.

Then I saw people tearing down those who wanted to make a difference. Those who stood up, some quaking in fear, but none the less, they stood, only to be mocked.

Again.

This is nothing new for women, people of color, LGBTQ or anyone else who doesn't fit the demographic the elusive and all-powerful 'they' feel is the 'right' one to be. What is new is people attacking other people of the same demographic. They can't understand what the big deal is, the world they live in isn't like that.

Good for them.

However, the rest of us can face hardships, daily simply for being who we are.

The divide in this country is widening at an alarming rate.

Again.

Instead of coming together we are bullying each other.

What are our kids learning?

The leader of this country can step up and close that gap. Bring this country together, to make a difference by unifying *all* people and not destroying this country from the inside out. This is where I have prayed my hardest that I was wrong because if I am right, this country will never be the same again.

I see economic ruin. The rich getting richer, while the lower and middle classes become one and all that remain is the top and bottom. Where our streets overflow with the homeless and children die from starvation. More than there already is.

I see discrimination the likes most of us have never witnessed, which considering what makes it on the news now, this is horrific future for the majority of the country.

I see women being fair game to every predator out there. I see them no longer having any control over their bodies or what is done to them.

I see higher insurance costs, assuming you can get any coverage.

I see drug prices climbing higher.

I see the mentally ill not being able to get the treatment they need.

I see elderly not being able to get the medications they need.

I see children dying because they can't get insurance because they have a preexisting condition and they are can't get approved for coverage.

I see where it is cheaper to die than to live.

I see children hurt because of the friends they keep. They see the worst in humanity, and it is only the beginning.

I see social anarchy, war, battles going on, and I can't get to my son in time to protect him.

I see the streets of my city burned out, a shell of what it used to be, the bombs dropping, the soldiers in the streets with automatic weapons.

I see my son being ripped out of my arms and put into military service at a young age, his innocence taken from him, his sweet personality crushed because foreign diplomacy is not part of this administration's priorities, and World War III has started.

At best, I see another civil war.

Let that sink in for a moment: the best-case scenario I can come up with is another civil war, because, at least then the rest of the world will be safe.

I hear the words said; I'm over reacting, blowing things out of proportion, emotional.

And I hear my voice, trying to speak, only to be told my opinion doesn't matter, or it is stupid. This is nothing new, I've heard it all my life.

I hear the cries of millions of people who just want a place to life, a job, and food for their family.

Basic unalienable rights.

Remember what this country was founded on.

We are all created equal.

We are all the same,

We all have hopes,

We all have dreams.

We all have strengths,

We all have weaknesses.

We all love,

We all hurt,

We all grieve.

We all protect,

We all nurture,

We all teach.

Remember what has come before, for surely history repeats itself.

Remember once some things are broken they can never be put back together.

Stop pointing fingers and learn how to work together to make this a better country.

For all.

Because if we don't, then that will mean I was right.

And I don't want to be.

qr

About the author:

M. Stratton has a beautifully twisted mind that will keep you on the edge of your seat, laughing and crying while you devour her books.

Author's website: www.mstrattonauthor.com

Remember

By Leslie Claire Walker

I don't remember the first article I read comparing the events during the 2016 U.S. election to those in 1933 Germany, but I remember what I felt as I read it: chilled to the marrow, with a sinking feeling in my gut and no small amount of fear.

Red flags rose high, flapping in the wind. Warning bells shook my bones.

The article distilled varied, yet thematically unified events into one chain of thought and action: *Create an enemy. Cast blame for the country's problems on that enemy. Teach the people to hate that enemy. Harm the enemy in whatever manner the people will allow.*

I never thought I would see such a thing in my lifetime. Not after the United States fought in a world war against the Nazis. Not after the establishment of the United States Holocaust Memorial Museum and many other remembrances. I should've known better.

Honestly, I did.

I just wanted a peaceful life. So, I pretended that what I saw and heard and read about was someone else's fault. That there was an enemy at the gates I could blame for all of it.

I conveniently categorized events as isolated incidents.

Each individual extrajudicial murder of a person of color. An uptick of antisemitism in parts of Europe, some of it violent. Genocide in other nations. The constant need during the Bush and Obama administrations to defend against those who would turn a war against terrorists into a war against all of Islam. Gay bashings. The murders of transwomen, particularly transwomen of color.

One that stands out may seem much less violent, much less a problem deserving attention than the others: the years' long campaign of insinuations and accusations that President Obama was born in Kenya and was a Muslim, rather than a Christian. Which really, of course, was meant to convey the idea that he is not one of us.

Who is "us?"

It became harder to pretend that these events were isolated, echoed as they were throughout the election.

A lifelong pattern of discrimination against Black people. The defamation of Mexican immigrants as rapists and criminals. Admitted sexual assault. Dog-whistles to white supremacists and white nationalists. Coy responses to questions from the media about an endorsement from the former Imperial Wizard of the Ku Klux Klan. A call for a total ban on the entry of Muslims into country.

I did not personally claim any of those thoughts or actions as my own, but I am as human as the people who did. I suppose it's better to awaken from pretending late than never to awaken at all, to acknowledge the beauty and terror of what it means to be a member of the human race.

We are who we are.

What does it mean to be tribal, as humans naturally are—and to be able to open our hearts and minds to our common humanity? What does it mean to be one of us?

I am a person of Jewish ancestry.

I was raised on stories of the 1939 voyage of the MS St. Louis, the German ocean liner whose captain, Gustav Schröder, tried to find homes for over 900 Jewish refugees from Germany. The refugees were denied entry into entry to Cuba, the U.S., and Canada. Fears that spies lurked among the refugees, that the refugees would take jobs that rightfully belonged to citizens, that the refugees were just too different—alien, other—spurred that denial. The refugees were sent back to Europe. Historians estimate that approximately a quarter of them died in death camps.

I remember them each time I hear people speak fearfully of possible terrorists among Syrian refugees. Of how different Muslim refugees are from the rest of us.

My family members, along with the others in the camps, were branded with numbers. Registered with the state that went about imprisoning, starving, and murdering them. I remember them when I hear calls for a Muslim registry.

My maternal grandfather fought in the Pacific during World War II. My maternal grandmother worked as part of the war effort at home, every day having to walk past the local headquarters of the Ku Klux Klan to do so. I wonder what they would think of what's happening today. Who would they count as one of us?

Create an enemy. Cast blame. Teach hate. Harm.

The same fears that doomed so many in the past, who like me—like all of us—only wanted to live peaceful lives, blossom over and over again, like poisonous flowers. We breathe in the deadly stuff. It enters our flesh and blood and bone. It becomes a part of us, but only if we allow it.

The Jewish people extol us never to forget the horrors of which humanity is—of which *we* are—capable. We say, "never again." Those are only words, unless we mean them with as much fierce love and commitment as we can muster. How do we reach fierce love? How do we reach commitment?

The millennia-long Jewish tradition of questioning holds a clue.

Who am I? What do I stand for? What am I willing to risk?

Those are easy questions during easy times, but they can become much harder to answer when enemies and blame and hate are the talk of the day, and holding onto peace becomes as difficult as trying to catch smoke with our bare hands.

There are no easy answers. Really, there is only one that matters.

A dear friend of mine always says, "Remember who you are."

Begin there. Here and now.

About the author:
Leslie Claire Walker grew up among the lush bayous of southeast Texas and currently lives in the Pacific Northwest with ornery cats, two harps, and too many fantasy novels to count. She is the author of the YA contemporary fantasy series The Faery Chronicles, including the novels HUNT, DEMON, and FAERY, and the Soul Forge urban fantasy series, beginning with NIGHT AWAKENS (2016) and NIGHT RISES (Summer 2017). Leslie takes her inspiration from the dark beauty of the city, the power of myth, and music ranging from Celtic harp to heavy metal. Even in the darkest of her tales, a spark lights the way.

Author's website: www.leslieclairewalker.com

My Immigrant Blood

By Zoe York

My grandfather was sixteen when he and his older brother were arrested by the Russians.

His father was killed.

His mother and younger brother fled Poland, making their way to Morocco, and then ports further afield. They ended up in Hong Kong for a period of time.

Nobody would take them for very long.

They were always in transit.

I was sixteen when I first talked about going to Poland to visit my grandparents' homeland. Dziadzio reminded me that where he was born is now in the Ukraine.

My grandfather was eighteen when the war shifted, and Russia and England struck a deal. Polish prisoners released, new pilots obtained. My grandfather went to England and learned how to fly a Lancaster bomber. He didn't speak much English, but it was a world war now, and the Canadians had sent translators. They were all in it together.

I was eighteen when Baba gave me an English-Polish dictionary.

My grandmother's parents immigrated to Canada when she was two. Their story is bleak; her mother committed suicide when my grandmother was twelve. She walked into the Red River in Winnipeg.

Depression runs like a ribbon through my immigrant blood, woven among strands of courage and adventure, new beginnings and heritage traditions. But immigrants know they must be grateful for what they have.

My grandmother escaped an unhappy childhood and seized an opportunity to serve in the war. She flew to England and translated Polish to English, and back again. She got married.

My grandmother was twenty-two when she returned to Canada with a Polish war groom.

I was twenty-two when I finally visited Auschwitz.

My grandfather was twenty-three when he became a farmer. It was all that was available to him in his new country. Immigrants know they must be grateful for what they have.

Potatoes, pigs, corn. Three children. He went back to school part-time. He'd always wanted to study mathematics.

I was twenty-three when I finished my degree. My grandfather paid for every cent of my tuition with money saved over fifty years of farming, even though my degree wasn't in math like his was. It was in Women's Studies, because my grandparents taught me about oppression and resistance, power and violence, and that human rights are sacrosanct.

This is what we do.

As human beings, this is what we do. We destroy, we rebuild, we move around the world. We raise families. And we resist.

We resist tyrants.

We resist fascists.

We resist racism, oppression, fear, hatred.

We are all refugees waiting to happen.

Note:
Almost everyone has a refugee story in their family tree. It might pre-date that word, but we're all connected by this global migration because of strife. When I hear criticism of people who get in boats, steal across borders, pay exorbitant amounts of money to get their children out of hellfire, I can't understand it. I would do anything and everything in my power to save my children from that, I would do exactly what they are doing, and exactly what my great-grandmothers did. I would travel the globe looking for a safe home for them, even if it took years. If you've read this far, I beg of you to please, try to understand how people fleeing a war zone are acting exactly as you would in the same situation.

qr

About the author:

Zoe York is a mother to two boys, a wife to a soldier, a very proud granddaughter, and a romance writer by trade. She lives in Canada, and travels the globe.

Author's website: www.zoeyork.com

One Hundred Percent of the Proceeds from the Sale of The Resistance United in Love will go to the American Civil Liberties Union.

The ACLU has been working to defend and preserve the individual rights and liberties guaranteed by the Constitution and laws of the United States for almost one hundred years.

https://www.aclu.org/

Thank you for reading our collection.

Treat others as you wish to be treated.

Give respect to earn respect.

United we stand, divided we fall.

Love trumps hate.

The Resistance Authors

Things you can do to make a difference

<u>Vote</u> – it is our right in the country, let your leaders know you are paying attention.

<u>Contact</u> – contact your representatives and leaders, let them know what you want for your city, state and national government. They are supposed to be our voice, let them know what to say.

<u>Run</u> – if you don't like how things are going, run for office. Start small, start large, but do something.

<u>Volunteer</u> – have a leader you admire and respect, volunteer to get the word out about them, share how they are making a difference.

<u>Charity</u> – there are thousands of charities that need help, either in your time or money. Do what you can to pay it forward. Be a helper in this world we live in.

<u>Respect</u> – respect our differences and learn from them.

When they go low, we go high

The Resistance Authors

Danielle Allen is a contemporary romance novelist and a diversity in romance advocate. She believes in spreading love, resisting hate, and standing up for what's right.

Author's website:
www.amazon.com/author/danielleallen

Dylan Allen is a Texas girl with a serious case of wanderlust. When she isn't writing or reading, eating or cooking, she and her family are planning their next adventure.

Author's website: www.authordylanallen.com

JC Andrijeski is a USA Today bestselling author of paranormal mystery, urban fantasy & supernatural suspense, often with a metaphysical bent. She's lived all over the United States as well as parts of Europe, Australia and Asia, and has a background in journalism and political history, with a Master's degree in the latter. She currently lives and writes full-time in Bangkok, Thailand, where she has a beautiful view of a Buddhist wat right outside her window.

Author's website: www.jcandrijeski.com

Megan Benjamin-Evans, author of Fleeting Heart: A Collection of Poetry, is a passionate poet and prolific audiobook narrator.

Author's website:
https://www.facebook.com/geekgirlwho/

Natasha Boyd is a first generation immigrant. Her grandfather helped Jews flee Denmark, her mother left South Africa's apartheid, and now she wonders if she'll be detained on her next trip back into the bastion of the "free world", the USA. She also writes about LOVE, and important, but forgotten, WOMEN IN HISTORY. She rarely writes poems. As you can probably tell.

Author's website: www.natashaboyd.com

Elizabeth Burgess lives with her partner in their beloved Louisiana. Her favorite things are writing about topics that make people blush, photography, and standing up for what's right. She also loves the color black.

Author's website: www.liddyburgess.com

Deborah Cunningham Burst is a New Orleans native who enjoys writing outdoors at her home in Mandeville, Louisiana. In her 15-year career as a freelance writer and photographer she has published more than 1,000 articles and twice as many photographs on a local, regional and national level. She has written four books in four years featuring historic churches and cemeteries.

Author's website: www.deborahburst.com

Emme Burton is the author of the Top 50 RomCom SNACK, the Better Than Series and AWKwaRd, Victoria. She wants you to #resist #persist and shop at Nordstrom.

Author's website: www.emmeburton.com

M.C. Cerny fell in love with books after experiencing her first real ugly cry reading, Where The Red Fern Grows. When M.C. is not writing, you'll find her lurking in Starbucks, running stupid marathon, singing Disney show tunes, and searching out the perfect shade of pink nail polish.

Author's website: www.authormccerny.com

SE Chardou is the author of romantic suspense and psychological romance. She also writes under the names of Selene Chardou and Elle Chardou.

Author's website:
www.facebook.com/Selene.chardou.and.elle.chardou

S. Simone Chavous is an International Best Selling paranormal and contemporary romance author. When she isn't writing, she enjoys reading, sketching, cooking, running, and spending time with family. She lives in northern Indiana with her family.

Author's website: www.ssimonechavous.com

T. Thorn Coyle is the author of "Like Water," the story collection "Alighting on His Shoulders" and the "The Panther Chronicles" series (Spring, 2017). She's also the author of multiple non-fiction books. A lifelong activist, she currently resides in the Pacific Northwest and drinks a lot of tea.

Author's website: www.thorncoyle.com

Sarah M. Cradit is the USA Today Bestselling Author of Southern Gothic Fantasy Fiction

Author's website: www.sarahmcradit.com

Ella Dominguez is a mother, lover, dreamer and bestselling author, Ella finds comfort in ukuleles and unicorns. An avid reader above all else, she takes pleasure in writing the stories that the characters in her head tell her to.

Author's link: Www.facebook.com/theartofsubmission

Nicole Falls is a contemporary Black romance writer who has taken entirely too long to complete her first project. She's also a ceramic mug and lapel pin enthusiast who cannot function without her wireless Beats constantly blaring music. When Nicole isn't writing, she spends her time trolling her friends and family while drinking coffee and/or cocktails or checking off yet another of these great United States visited in her quest to see some land! She currently resides in the suburbs of Chicago.

Author's website: http://www.nicolefalls.com/books/

John Gregory Hancock is a storyteller, a graphic artist and a patriot who cares deeply about this country.

Author's website:
http://www.johngregoryhancock.com/

Bayli Lane is an animal lover, social activist, and contemporary romance author.

Author's website:
https://www.goodreads.com/authorbaylilane

Robin Lee is a Snarky Southern lady who likes to wax poetic and sprinkle her prose with a pinch of sugar and a dash of spice. Author of Bittersweet Illusion, a poetry collection, and the upcoming novel Playing Dirty.

Author's website: www.ugly-beautiful.com

Olivia Linden was born in New York, but raised in both Queens, NY and San Antonio, TX. As a shy young girl, writing was her creative outlet. Mini plays, short stories, poems and even a few comic strips were created from her love of writing and reading books. She also loves to blog about relationships and social issues when she has the time.

Author's website: http://www.vialinden.com/

Harper Miller is a thirty-something native New Yorker. She's traveled the world and lived in a variety of places but always finds her way back to the Big Apple. A lackluster love life leaves time to explore new interests; for Harper it is writing. *The Sweetest Taboo: An Unconventional Romance* is her debut novel. In her mind, the perfect Alpha male possesses intellect, humor, and a kinky streak that rivals the size of California.

When she isn't writing, Harper utilizes her graduate degree in the field of medical research. She enjoys fitness-related activities, drinking copious amounts of wine, and going on bad dates.

Author's website: www.authorharpermiller.com

G.Miller is a journalist and fiction writer from Connecticut who writes about sports, race, and culture. He has written four novels and contributed to sports and politics stories for USA Today and OZY.

Author's website: www.noapologiesnation.com

Morgan Jane Mitchell is a bestselling erotic romance and paranormal author, Morgan Jane Mitchell spent years blogging politics and health trends before she rediscovered her love of writing fiction. Trading politicians for bloodsuckers of another kind, she's now the author of bestselling post-apocalyptic fantasy novel, Sanguis City.

Author's website: www.themorganjane.com

Katherine Rhodes is a lackadaisical laundry goddess, and an expert in the profundities of bad music and awful literature-thanks to her husband-Katherine strives to find balance in the universe and time to cook dinner.

Author's website: www.Katherinerhodes.com

C. Ricketts is an Indie Author of romance, but love my insanely suspenseful romances the best. Mother, wife, reader & I knit, but not at the same time. Mentally writing my life story, but it's an organic work of art so remains incomplete.

Author's website: www.smexyindieauthor.com

Kimberly Rose lives on the island of Oahu for now, until her husband's career in the Navy moves them again. A lover of the written word she enjoys reading, writing, and teaching Language Arts.

Author's website:
www.authorkimberlyrose.wordpress.com

Amalie Silver resides in Minnesota with her husband, two toddlers, and black cat, Mr. Fish. She consumes approximately three pots of coffee a day, and credits this for her survival over the past decade.

Author's website: https://amaliesilver.wordpress.com/

M. Stratton has a beautifully twisted mind that will keep you on the edge of your seat, laughing and crying while you devour her books.

Author's website: www.mstrattonauthor.com

Leslie Claire Walker grew up among the lush bayous of southeast Texas and currently lives in the Pacific Northwest with ornery cats, two harps, and too many fantasy novels to count. She is the author of the YA contemporary fantasy series The Faery Chronicles, including the novels HUNT, DEMON, and FAERY, and the Soul Forge urban fantasy series, beginning with NIGHT AWAKENS (2016) and NIGHT RISES (Summer 2017). Leslie takes her inspiration from the dark beauty of the city, the power of myth, and music ranging from Celtic harp to heavy metal. Even in the darkest of her tales, a spark lights the way.

Author's website: www.leslieclairewalker.com

Zoe York is a mother to two boys, a wife to a soldier, a very proud granddaughter, and a romance writer by trade. She lives in Canada, and travels the globe.

Author's website: www.zoeyork.com